HOW JUSTICE GREW

Virginia Counties: An Abstract of Their Formation

MARTHA W. HIDEN

The University Press of Virginia

Charlottesville

Jamestown 350th Anniversary
Historical Booklet, Number 19

HOW JUSTICE GREW

Virginia Counties: An Abstract of Their Formation

In addition to their human cargo, the poultry and fruit acquired in the West Indies, the clothing, household gear, and other possessions of the passengers, the *Susan Constant, Godspeed* and *Discovery* had a large though imponderable cargo of English laws, customs and religion. The colonists had left England, neither driven out nor seeking escape, but to found a new England in a new world.

Though the seat of government was at "King James His Towne," the natural curiosity to explore and the economic necessity for means of livelihood caused settlements to spring up farther and farther away. Despite the fact that the colonists were in a region where rivers and numerous streams afforded easy transportation interrupted only for short periods by ice in winter, attendance at court in Jamestown was burdensome.

THE FOUR CORPORATIONS

By 17 June 1617, Governor Samuel Argall had established the four great divisions of the colony, namely: "the incorporations and parishes of James City, Charles City, Henrico and Kikotan" (later Elizabeth City). The Eastern Shore settlements were not included in this division.

Each of the incorporations mentioned above and the Eastern Shore contained one or more boroughs or settlements. Eleven of the settlements in the four incorporations were represented by two Burgesses each, in the first General Assembly. This, the first legislative assembly of English speaking people in the West-

1

ern hemisphere, convened on 30 July 1619 in the church at Jamestown. Itself based on the English Parliament as a model, it became the model followed by all succeeding British colonies including Australia. The colonial assembly next in age to Virginia's is that of Bermuda established in 1620. In the *Journals of the House of Burgesses*, the names of the Burgesses for the 1619 Assembly are arranged by the cities and plantations they represented. In the Journal of the second Assembly that is extant, 1623/24, for the first and only time, the plantations are grouped under the corporations of which they were a part, except Eastern Shore, which, as has been noted, was a separate entity.

In 1621, a charter from the Company confirmed former grants and provided "that the Governor should call the General Assembly once a year, and initiate the policy of the form of government, laws, customs, manner of trial and other administration of justice used in England." Governor Wyatt at the same time was ordered to make arrangements for "dividing the colony into cities, boroughs, etc., . . . and to appoint proper times for administration . . . and law suits." William Stith in his *History of Virginia* states: "Inferior courts were therefore in the beginning of the year 1621 appointed in convenient places to relieve the Governor and Council of the vast burthen of business and to render justice more cheap and accessible. This was the original and foundation of our County Courts, although the country was not yet laid off in counties."

The General Assembly of 1623/24 provided "that there shall be courts kept once a month in the corporations of Charles City and Elizabeth City for the deciding of suits and controversies not exceeding the value of one hundred pounds of tobacco and for punishing of petty offenses." As a consequence of this act, the question of the metes and bounds of these corporations, Charles City, Henrico, Elizabeth City and James City, became important, since suits must perforce be instituted in the court having juris-

2

diction over that particular area. Mr. Nathaniel C. Hale, in his interesting book on William Claiborne called *Virginia Venturer*, shows that William Claiborne in 1621, was appointed a surveyor for the colony and comments that heretofore boundaries of land had been located with ungraduated mariners' compasses and described by careless references to natural limits.

Apparently the Jamestown Court with those of Charles City and Elizabeth City was adequate for several years, but in February 1631/32 the Assembly passed an act adding five more as follows: "for the upper parts"; "for Warwick River; for Warrosquyoake; for Elizabeth City; for Accawmacke." Presumably, since the order had been that the new courts were to be held "in remote parts of the colony," the phrase "upper parts" would mean the most western part of Henrico Corporation, and the Elizabeth City Court would be for the south side of Hampton Roads. This seems logical since the north side had been settled first, was more populous and was not remote from Jamestown.

THE EIGHT ORIGINAL SHIRES

But the colony was growing too fast for this arrangement to continue adequate for long. With a population of about 5,000 persons, the time for division into shires or counties was at hand. It may be noted that, though these units were designated as shires in the Act of the General Assembly creating them, they were, after that, always called counties. Their functions were the same as those of their English prototypes, but conditions here required two changes which will be mentioned later.

The names of the four corporations, Charles City, Henrico, James City and Elizabeth City were kept for four of the newly created counties, but their areas were lessened. The four new divisions were: Warwick River, later called Warwick; Warrosquyoake, later Isle of Wight; Charles River, later changed to York, and Accomack which embraced all the settlements on the Eastern Shore of Virginia.

3

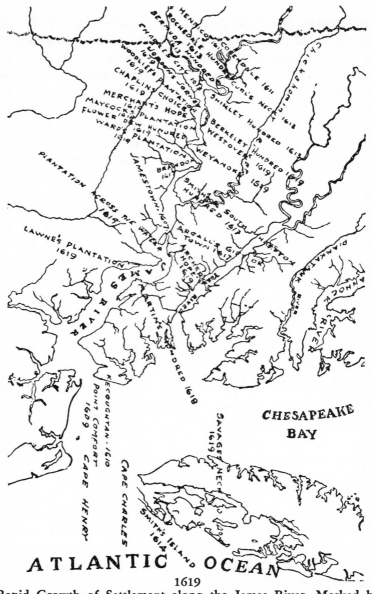

1619

Rapid Growth of Settlement along the James River. Marked by
Introduction of Representative Government.

The tender feeling for the homeland is evidenced by the fact that six out of the "eight original shires," as they are generally called, bore names reminiscent of England. Henrico perpetuated Henry, Prince of Wales, son of James I whose early death made even more difficult the first years of the Colony. Charles City honored his brother Charles, later Charles I, who combined, to his undoing, the charm and obstinacy of the Stuarts. Elizabeth City and the river of the same name derive from Princess Elizabeth, the oldest sister of Henry and Charles. She married Frederick, for a time King of Bohemia, but later overthrown and exiled. Though her life was bitter and tragic, her descendants since 1714 have occupied the throne of Britain. James City was, of course, for King James I, of whom it was said that his instructors had given him an abundance of knowledge but had been unable to give him sense. Warwick's name was for Robert Rich, Earl of Warwick, leader of one of the factions of the Virginia Company, who had founded and cared for the colony. He belonged to the "Court Party" which wished to continue martial law in the colony and opposed the liberal views of Sir Edwin Sandys and the Earl of Southampton. For awhile the Sandys faction was in control and the "Great Charter of Laws, Orders and Privileges" brought over by Sir George Yeardley was the expression of their views on colonial government. But the "Court Party" prevailed in the end and the charter of the Virginia Company was revoked in 1624. Charles River County presumably took its name from Charles I, who was King when it was formed. In 1642/43 when it became York, the change was made to honor James, the second son of Charles I, who in that year was created Duke of York. Warrosquyoake, an Indian word, was later Isle of Wight County since some of its most prominent residents were from the small island of that name lying off the English coast. The Parish lying in and coterminous with Isle of Wight County was called Newport from the largest city in the English island.

5

Accomack honored the friendly tribe of Indians of that name residing on the Eastern Shore.

The bounds of these eight counties as noted in Tyler's *The Cradle of the Republic* were as follows:

Elizabeth City County extending on both sides of Hampton Roads, on the south side to Chuckatuck Creek and on the north side to Newport News and including a small part thereof.

Warrosquyoake County, later Isle of Wight, extending on the south side of James River from Chuckatuck Creek to Lawne's Creek.

Warwick River County extending on the north side of James River from Elizabeth City County to Skiffe's (Keith's) Creek. This is the only original shire from which no other county was formed. The name was changed to Warwick County in 1643.

James City County extending on both sides of James River, on the south side from Lawne's Creek to Upper Chippokes Creek and on the north side from Skiffe's Creek to above Sandy Point.

Charles City County also extending on both sides of James River, on the south side from Upper Chippokes Creek to Appomattox River and on the north side from Sandy Point to Turkey Island Creek.

Henrico County extending from Charles City County on both sides of James River indefinitely westward.

Charles River County, later York, lay to the north of Warwick County and adjoined Elizabeth City County on the east. Its north and west boundaries were indefinite. The colonists soon crossed the York River to establish plantations along its northern bank and settled as far west as the Pamunkey River.

Accomack, the eighth shire, like York County, showed the vitality of the colonists in pushing settlements away from the vicinity of Jamestown into uncharted wilds.

The Potomac River was the dividing line between Virginia

6

and Maryland, and on the Eastern Shore the division was approximately in line with the mouth of this river. Settling on the Shore in 1616, the colonists moved slowly northward. The Indians were friendly, transportation easy, climate mild, and soil fertile. There was no impediment to growth.

The population of the colony is estimated to have been around 5,000 persons in 1634 as has been noted. Six years later it had increased about 50%, being 7,466 persons. One factor in this growth was the unrest in England at this time which culminated a few years later in bitter civil war.

THE COLONIAL COURTS

We have mentioned that the creation of counties with their courts had in view to render justice more accessible to all. There were by 1642, in the colony six kinds of courts for the administration of justice.

The first of these was the magistrate's court. In 1642, an Act of the Assembly empowered a magistrate or justice to try a case involving not over twenty shillings in currency or 200 pounds of tobacco in value. In 1657/58, the amount could be as much as 1,000 pounds of tobacco if two magistrates were present but only 350 pounds if but one magistrate tried the case. The appeal from the magistrate's court was to the monthly court.

The next court was the parish court. In the seventeenth century only one of these courts existed in Virginia and that only for a short time. This was the court of Bristol Parish which most likely sat in the old Merchants Hope Church, still standing and still in use. The court was discontinued before the end of the seventeenth century, and its papers passed into the custody of the Henrico County Court. A parish court was in a way a vestigial body, a relic of days when the authority of the church was preeminent in both civil and ecclesiastical matters.

The third recourse for justice was to the monthly court, developed according to Stith, from the inferior court established

7

in 1621. The Governor named the first justices of a new county, renamed justices in the old counties and filled every vacancy as it occurred. By Act of Assembly in 1628/29, the number of justices was to be eight, but later it was increased to ten. Four constituted a quorum. Three other members of the bench associated with one member of the quorum, who had a different status from the other justices, formed a sufficient number to make a valid court. The person whose name appeared at the head of the list of those constituting the quorum probably served as presiding justice; in his absence, the one named second and so on down the list. No pay was provided for the justices.

In 1642, the Assembly ordered that at least six monthly courts be held every year and the justices were empowered to determine when extra sessions were necessary. At the same time, another Act of Assembly provided that Henrico should hold court on the first day of every month; Charles City on the third; James City on the sixth; Isle of Wight on the ninth; Upper Norfolk (later Nansemond) on the twelfth; Elizabeth City on the eighteenth; Warwick on the twenty-first; York on the twenty-fourth; and Northampton, (formerly Accomack) on the twenty-eighth. The careful spacing between these courts enabled attorneys to appear in cases in different counties with no conflict of dates.

The range of cases that could come before a monthly court was naturally wider than could come before a magistrate. As much as ten pounds sterling could be involved in a suit and there was no appeal from the decision; when larger amounts were involved, the defeated litigant could appeal to the General Court. All questions where injury to life or limb was at stake went before the General Court.

The monthly county courts had, in a general way, a jurisdiction resembling the combined jurisdiction of the English Chancery Court, King's Bench, Common Pleas, Court Exchequer, Admiralty and Ecclesiastical. The justices of the monthly courts looked after the poor and afflicted, held special orphan courts at least once a year, granted probates of wills, passed on appraisements of estates as presented to them for inspection, on inventories and estate accounts which also were presented for their scrutiny, and recorded conveyances of land.

Recordation of land conveyances is one of the two differences between the monthly court of a Virginia county and its British prototype. There conveyances were private property and retained in private ownership. Manor houses of old English estates often had a room called the "Muniment room" where deeds, inventories, rent rolls and such family papers, often including copies of wills, were kept. The name derived from a Latin word meaning to fortify or strengthen, since the deeds strengthened the validity of ownership claimed by the holder of the land. The other function of the monthly court in Virginia different from the English Shire Court was the power to probate wills. In England probate of wills was in the prerogative courts of Canterbury and York. Probably since there was no diocesan see in Virginia, Virginia being in the diocese of London, the monthly court offered the most feasible place of probate.

It has been noted that there was a limit to the powers of this court and that cases which it could not hear went before the General Court. This court was composed of the Governor and his Council of State. It met semi-annually, 15 April and 15 October, each term lasting at least eighteen days. The Governor presided at these sessions. The presence of five members was necessary for the transaction of business. The *Minutes of the Council and General Court* are extant for the years 1622-1632 and abstracts for the years 1670-1676. They were published in one volume by the Virginia State Library in 1924 and are helpful in acquiring a general picture of life in the colony in the seventeenth century.

The General Assembly was also a judicial body with power to render decisions. At its afternoon session the 22nd day of September 1674, a cause came before the Council and General

Court which had originated in Accomack County. The Court made no decision but ordered it "referred to the Assembly by reason it very much concern the country." From that one would infer that causes involving general principles were deemed proper for discussion and decision by the Burgesses who represented the entire colony, since all would be affected by the decision.

The Court of Admiralty, the last dispenser of justice in the colony, seems to have been established about 1697 under the governorship of Sir Edmund Andros. Previously such matters as would come within the province of this court had been handled by other judicial procedures, as they were later. The instances of piracy were not numerous enough to justify the maintenance of a Court of Admiralty in Virginia. No records of this court survive.

It may seem we have wandered far from the formation of counties, but since the accessibility of justice for all was a prime consideration in their creation, it would appear well to examine the means by which the average citizen could have his grievances heard and decided. The importance of the county monthly court in his life cannot be overestimated. While on business at court, he had opportunity to see his friends, play cards, gamble, race horses, fight, drink, "swap" horses and other livestock, attend the muster of county militia to which he belonged, and see the newest articles imported from England. The county court and his parish church services were his chief contacts with the world that lay beyond his plantation.

"Justice Accessible to All." County Divisions Begin

Scarcely had the eight original counties begun to function before the expansion of population forced the erection of a new one. In 1636 that part of Elizabeth City County lying on the south side of Hampton Roads became a separate entity under the name of New Norfolk, a name probably derived from the English shire. No court records of this year survive. The next year 1637, New Norfolk itself was divided into Lower Norfolk and Upper Norfolk counties.

Also in 1637, Warrosquyoake County lost its Indian name, becoming Isle of Wight. By Act of Assembly passed in January 1639/40, the bounds between these three counties were set as follows: Isle of Wight to begin at Lawne's Creek, thence down the main river to Richard Hays's, formerly John Seaward's, including the said plantation and families and from thence from the main river into the woods southerly to the plantation of William Nowell and Mr. Robert Pitt, with the said plantation and families, and thence south as aforesaid. The Upper County of New Norfolk to begin at the aforesaid plantation of Richard Haies, from thence southerly into the woods as aforesaid, and by the main river, from thence to extend down by the main river unto the creek near the plantation of Francis Bullock being the first creek to the westward of Crany Point including the plantation of the said Francis Bullock and no ways intrenching upon the Western Branch of Elizabeth River nor the creek thereof which do belong to the county of Lower Norfolk. The parishes in these counties were ordered to be coterminous with the bounds of the counties. Upper Norfolk County kept its name only a few years; in March 1645/46, the Assembly directed it should "be from henceforth nominated and called county of Nansemun."

INDIAN DISTRICT CHICKACOAN BECOMES NORTHUMBERLAND

Whether because of the Puritan element in Nansemond or because of Quakers resident there, who on account of their aversion to war were of no aid against the Indians, settlement for the first time turned away from Tidewater to the area lying between the Rappahannock and the Potomac Rivers. Because of its fertile soil, easy transportation and healthful climate, the colonists patented land in this favored region in increasing numbers. By 1645 the county of Northumberland had been formed and organized. Although we have no Act of Assembly to estab-

11

lish the date of its formation, an item from a volume of *Maryland Archives* under date of 1645 referring to Lieutenant Colonel John Trussell of the county of Northumberland shows the county was then functioning.

The area from which Northumberland was formed had borne the Indian name of Chickacoan. It was a border settlement with no stable government and in need of law and order. Northumberland extended from the Potomac to and across the Rappahannock River and from the tip of "Northern Neck," as the territory lying between the two rivers was called, indefinitely westward. The name derives from the English shire, Northumberland.

Population of the colony is estimated to have been about 15,000 in 1649, 500 of whom were negroes, and in 1654, 21,600 persons. This rapid growth was due largely to the Civil War in England which made Virginia a haven of refuge for many.

NORTHUMBERLAND DIVIDED

In 1651, that portion of Northumberland lying on both sides of the Rappahannock River was divided and a new county, called Lancaster from the English shire of that name, was formed.

Colonists were moving westward in Northumberland and the distance to its courthouse made attendance at court difficult. In 1653, the new county of Westmoreland was set up from the western end of Northumberland to take care of these new residents. Its boundaries were "from Machoatoke River where Mr. Cole lives and so upwards to the falls of the great river of Potomac above the Necostins Town." It did not extend across the Rappahannock River. The "Mr. Cole" referred to is probably the Richard Cole, who in his will, directed that an elaborate tombstone be ordered for him carrying the following inscription:

"Here lies Dick Cole a grievous sinner
Who died shortly before dinner
Yet hopes in Heaven to find a place
To satiate his soul with grace."

12

Westmoreland, destined to share with Charles City County the destinction of being the birthplace of two Presidents of the United States, is a beautifully situated area with famous estates on its fertile lands. Among these should be mentioned "Stratford," the birthplace of two Signers of the Declaration of Independence, Richard Lee and Francis Lightfoot Lee, and of General Robert E. Lee.

NEW TIDEWATER COUNTIES

Leaving the rapidly growing Northern Neck of Virginia, we return to the Tidewater area to see the developments there. Just as the 1622 Massacre had retarded settlements on the south bank of the York River, so the 1644 Massacre had delayed expansion on the north side of the York. Although in 1648 a petition was presented to the Assembly reciting "the great and clamorous necessities of divers of the inhabitants occasioned and brought upon them through the mean produce of their labours upon barren and over-wrought grounds" and praying leave to settle on the north side of Charles (York) and Rappahannock Rivers, the Assembly postponed the date of such settlement until 1 September 1649. It seems to have been about two years later, 1651, before Gloucester County was established, and Burgesses from the new county are first listed in April 1652.

It may be mentioned that this is an early example of the cause underlying a great deal of the migration in Virginia: "barren and over-wrought grounds," the toll that tobacco yearly exacted from the soil and the continuing need for new land to cultivate in order to produce profitable crops of tobacco.

Only a little later than the northward expansion of York, evidenced by the new county of Gloucester, came its growth to the west. In 1654, Captain Robert Abrell appeared in the Assembly as Burgess from New Kent County. Like Gloucester, it derived from an English shire of the same name, and was bestowed in honor of Colonel William Claiborne of Crayford, Kent, Eng-

13

land, at this date a distinguished resident of the new county. Its bounds were "from the west side of Skimeno Creek to the heads of Pamunkey and Mattapony Rivers and down to the head of the west side of Poropotank Creek."

Expansion also had taken place on the south side of James River directly across from Jamestown. The easterly bound of James City across the river was Lawne's Creek established in 1634 when the county of Warrosquyoake (Isle of Wight) was formed. The west boundary on the south side of the river was Upper Chippokes Creek. This, too, had been set up in 1634. Now in 1652, this area lying between these two creeks became Surry. Though named for the English shire, the spelling of the Virginia county has always omitted the "e" the English Surrey uses. It is said the name was selected because Surrey in England has the same geographical position to London as the Virginia Surry has to Jamestown, then the seat of government.

With the formation of Surry County the needs of the population were satisfied for exactly 51 years. Not until 1703 was another south side division needed.

The Northern Neck and The Eastern Shore Divide

Not so along the Rappahannock, for by 1656 only three years after Westmoreland was created, a petition was presented to the Assembly by "the inhabitants of the lower part of Lancaster County showing their vast distance from the county courts" and praying that a division be made. The Assembly acceded to their wishes, ordering "the upper part of Mr. Bennett's land known by the name of Naemhock on the south side of the easternmost branch of Morattico Creek on the north side the river be the lowermost bounds of the upper county; the lower county to retain the name of Lancaster and the upper county to be named Rappahannock County." This division followed the bounds of two parishes previously established.

14

King William County Courthouse, King William, Virginia

Hanover County Courthouse, Hanover, Virginia

Virginia State Chamber of Commerce

Isle of Wight County Clerk's Office, Isle of Wight, Virginia

The formation of Rappahannock County in 1656 ended the list of counties formed in the decade 1650 to 1660.

The next development was on the Eastern Shore. It had become sufficiently populous to support two county governments and in an Act of the Assembly March 1661/62 reference is made to the two counties. The southern part of the peninsula retained the name it had borne for twenty years, Northampton, and the county to the north assumed the name once borne by the entire peninsula, Accomack. The question of the boundary line between the two divisions dragged on for twenty-five years, being settled 22 March 1687/88. It has remained fixed. The boundary between Virginia and Maryland also was long in dispute, but Watkins Point at the mouth of Pocomoke River on its north side is the western end of the line. The line across the peninsula was set at a little north of the point.

With Eastern Shore divided into two counties, no further growth was possible and the peninsula remains two counties.

The next county to be formed in the colony was Stafford, which lies on the north side of the Rappahannock River to the west of Westmoreland. The name is in honor of an English shire. When formed in 1664, it was a border county with constant fear of Indian attacks since an established Indian trail regularly used by their hunting parties lay within its territory. Its north and west boundaries were not well defined, but included the area later Fairfax, Prince William, Fauquier, Loudoun and Alexandria (now Arlington) Counties.

Middlesex County, next to be noted, was functioning as a county in 1669 as Mr. F. W. Sydnor demonstrated in an article in *Virginia Magazine of History and Biography*, Volume 42. It was taken from Lancaster County, being the portion that lies on the south side of the Rappahannock River and extends to Dragon Run, the northern boundary of Gloucester. It had been the southern part of Christ Church Parish in Lancaster and retained the same parish name. Christ Church was the only parish and co-

15

terminous with Middlesex County. By good fortune, Christ Church in Lancaster and Christ Church in Middlesex are still preserved and in use. Both the Register and Vestry Book of the latter have survived the years, the former begins in 1653 and the latter ten years later. No Register of Christ Church Lancaster survives, and the extant Vestry Book covers only the years 1739 to 1786. Middlesex, never large, was, in colonial days, the home of numerous distinguished families, among them the Wormeleys, whose house "Rosegill" has seen many important historical events. The name Middlesex is for the English shire, doubtless the birthplace of many early residents of the Virginia County.

THE COLONY PROSPERS UNDER A KING AND QUEEN AND TWO NEW COUNTIES HONOR THE ROYAL FAMILY

After Middlesex in 1669, there was a hiatus of 22 years before a new county was created. In that period, the colony's fortunes had been checkered, and unrest and depression had been widespread. Troubles with the Indians, Bacon's Rebellion and economic ills, which led to tobacco cutting, all combined to make Virginia a gloomy place. The accession of James II brought no improvement in England, and the time was ripe for revolution. James II was forced to flee. He was succeeded by his daughter Mary and her husband, who was his nephew, Prince William of Orange. Under their rule, both England and Virginia became more prosperous. The next new county, King and Queen, created 1691, was named in their honor. This was formed from New Kent, "so that Pamunkey River divide the same, and so down York River to the extent of the county, and that the part which is now on the south side of York and Pamunkey River be called New Kent, and the north side with Pamunkey Neck be called and known by the name of King and Queen county." It was enacted further "that the inhabitants of Pamunkey Neck, that now belong to St. Peter's Parish be restored and added to St. John's Parish from which they formerly were taken, and

16

that the Pamunkey River be the bounds betwixt the two parishes."

About the same time Lower Norfolk became populous enough to justify the formation of a new county. This was to begin "at the new inlet of Little Creek and so up the said creek to the dams between Jacob Johnson and Richard Drout and so out of the said dams up a branch the head of which branch lyeth between the dwelling house of William Moseley, Senr., and the new dwelling house of Edmond Webb, and so to run from the head of the said branch on a direct line to the dams at the head of the Eastern branch of Elizabeth River, the which dams lie between James Kemp and Thomas Ivy, and so down the said branch to the mouth of a small branch or gutt that divides the land which Mr. John Porter now lives on from the land he formerly lived on, and so up the said small branch according to the bounds of the said plantation where the said Porter now liveth, and from thence to the great swamp that lieth on the east side of John Showlands and so along the said great swamp to the North River of Currituck and down the said North River to the mouth of Simpson's Creek and so up the said creek to the head thereof and from thence by a south line to the bounds of Carolina." The name of this new division was Princess Anne honoring the second daughter of James II by his first wife Anne Hyde, and the sister of Queen Mary. Later Princess Anne became a very popular Queen, Fluvanna County, the Rivanna River, the North Anna and South Anna and the Rapidan River all being named for her. At the same time that Princess Anne was formed, the name of Lower Norfolk was changed to Norfolk County.

Richmond and Essex From Old Rappahannock

Settlers had long found the Rappahannock River area attractive. The county of this name, established in 1656, and lying on both sides of the river, had grown steadily and its population was sufficient to support two county governments. It was enacted that the river be the dividing line, "that part which is now on the north side thereof be called and known by the name Richmond County and that that which is now on the south side thereof be called and known by the name of Essex County." It was further ordered "that the records belonging to the county court of Rappahannock before this division be kept in Essex County, that belonging wholly to their majesties and the other to the proprietors of the North Neck." This was a seemingly casual reference to the grant Charles II had made to some of his supporters while he was in exile and had confirmed on his coming to the throne; it comprised over five million acres lying between the Potomac and Rappahannock Rivers from their headsprings to the Chesapeake Bay. Not until the colony became independent was the Proprietary abolished.

In 1702 another division was created. The land lying between the Pamunkey and Mattaponi Rivers, known as Pamunkey Neck was taken from King and Queen and became King William County. This honored the reigning monarch, King William, now a widower since the death of Queen Mary in 1694.

King William died the same year his namesake county was formed and his sister-in-law, Queen Anne came to the throne. The first county formed thereafter honored her husband, the Prince Consort, George of Denmark. The new county, Prince George, embraced that portion of Charles City lying on the south side of James River. The estate, "Brandon," and the third oldest church building in Virginia known as Merchants Hope, are within its confines.

After a reign of twelve years Queen Anne died and the Elector of Hanover ascended the throne as King George I of England. Several years before this, the Tangier-born Alexander Spotswood was appointed Lieutenant Governor of Virginia and took up his residence in Williamsburg. Williamsburg had become the capital in 1699. It was on higher land than malarial Jamestown and a more healthful place to live.

Governor Spotswood was active and eager to explore the re-

18

sources of the colony. One of his achievements was to lead a group of adventurous persons to the summit of the Blue Ridge and blaze the way for westward expansion. He also was interested in bringing over from the German Palatinate colonists adept in iron mining, and establishing them on the edges of older settlements. This brought about the creation of several counties as we shall see later.

In 1721 the "Upper Inhabitants" of Richmond County because of their great distance from the courthouse petitioned to become a separate county. The eastern part lying below "Charles Beaver Dams and from the head thereof by a north course to Westmoreland County" was to retain the name Richmond and the part above the said dams and course was to be King George County. The name, of course, honored George I.

When New Kent was formed in 1654 its western bounds were indefinite. By 1721, however, the "Upper Inhabitants" of this county were sufficiently numerous to petition for division on account of their great distance from court. It was ordered that "that part of the county lying below the Parish of St. Paul" was to remain New Kent and the part lying in St. Paul's Parish was to be known as Hanover County. The name again honors the reigning monarch.

Also in 1721, a third new county was formed and called Spotsylvania for the energetic and capable Governor. Spotsylvania was taken from Essex, and parts of King and Queen and King William. The bounds of Spotsylvania specifically laid out in the Act creating it were "upon Snow Creek up to the mill, thence by a southwest line to the river, North Anna, thence up the river as far as convenient and thence by a line to be run over the high mountains to the river on the northwest side thereof, so as to include the northern passage through the said mountains, thence down the said river until it comes against the head of Rappahannock thence, by a line to the head of Rappahannock River; and down that river to the mouth of Snow Creek." Within the portion of Spotsylvania that was taken from Essex, the Governor, some years before, had located a group of German immigrants at a place called Germanna on the Rapidan River.

Besides the Germans, there was a group of Huguenots who had come over a few years earlier and settled on the James River some 20 miles above the Falls. There were also immigrants, both from England and Scotland, who were loyal to the Stuart cause, and its leader, James, son of James II by his second wife, Mary of Modena. The rising of the Scotch clans in his favor in 1715 was crushed by the battle of Preston. Many of the captured Highlanders were deported to America and others, fearing capture, emigrated. These three new factors in the life of the colony are worthy of notice.

In 1727/28, an Act was passed by the Assembly to take effect the next year dividing the county of Henrico. The division was to be "by a line on the north side James River beginning at the mouth of Tuckahoe Creek thence up the said creek to Chumley's Branch thence along a line of marked trees north twenty degrees east to Hanover County and on the south side James River beginning at the Lower Manachin Creek from thence along a line of marked trees in a direct course to the mouth of Skinquarter Creek on Appomattox River." The land to the east of this line was to remain Henrico and that to the west to comprise the new county of Goochland. Sir William Gooch had become Lieutenant Governor of Virginia in 1727 and served 22 years. He was probably the most popular of the colonial governors, seemingly able to work harmoniously with the Council which was necessary for success.

At the same time that Goochland was formed another new county came into being. This was described in the bill brought before the House of Burgesses as "An act for erecting a new county on the heads of Essex, King and Queen and King William Counties and for calling the same Caroline County." The name derives from Caroline of Anspach, Queen of George II who had succeeded his father, George I as King the year before. It will be recalled that Queen Caroline gave money to Thomas Lee to aid him in building "Stratford" when his former house had been burned by criminals whom he, as a magistrate, had sentenced for their misdeeds. Caroline County was not an expansion of settlements as most of the other counties had been for it was bounded completely by already established governments. Its creation, however, was in line with the thesis already laid down "to make justice accessible to all", and made court attendance more convenient for dwellers in the northwest portions of Essex, King and Queen and King William.

Three years later, in 1731, a new county was created from the northwest portions of Stafford and King George "above Choppawomsick Creek on Potomac River and Deep Creek on Rappahannock River and a southwest line to be made from the head of the north branch of the said creek to the head of the said Deep Run." This area was to be known as Prince William County honoring by this title, William Augustus, Duke of Cumberland, the King's brother. He was later known as "The Butcher of Culloden" because of the ferocity of his treatment of the Scotch Highlanders after the battle of Culladen in 1745. This battle, so sanguinary and devastating in its effects, wiped out the Stuart sympathizers and there were no further attempts to depose the Hanoverian dynasty from the British throne. The county seat is Manassas, near which were fought two battles of the Civil War.

Brunswick and Migration Southward

In 1720, the Assembly passed an act to be effective in 1721, creating Spotsylvania County as has been mentioned. At the same time, there was an act to form a county from the southern part of Prince George County and name it Brunswick for the Duchy of Brunswick which was then a possession of the Electorate of Hanover. The description is as follows: that Brunswick County should

21

begin "on the south side of the River Roanoke at the place where the line lately run for ascertaining the uncontroverted bounds of this colony towards North Carolina intersects the said river Roanoke and to be bounded by the direction of the governor with consent of council so as to include the southern pass." No steps were taken for carrying out this act because of the small number of settlers in the area, until May 1732, when it was enacted that the earlier legislation become effective the first of January ensuing. Setting up the county government had been made possible by adding parts of Surry and Isle of Wight, thus increasing the the number of tithables and lessening the amount of taxes each would pay. The preamble to the act expresses this thought in more precise phrase when it says "whereas by reason of the small number of tithables in the county of Brunswick the poll taxes must necessarily be very grievous and burthensome to them, which by an addition of parts of the counties of Surry and Isle of Wight would be remedied, and divers of the inhabitants of the two last mentioned counties would thereby also be freed from hardships and inconveniences which at present they labour under."

The reference to the line lately run "between Virginia and North Carolina" is the famous survey made by Col. William Byrd, Major William Mayo, John Irvine and others which forms the subject of *The History of the Dividing Line* written by Colonel Byrd. The Mayo River in Patrick and Henry Counties perpetuates the name of Major Mayo, the skilled surveyor in the party. The entire boundary was not surveyed then, in fact it was a good many years later before it was necessary to have a clear limit between the two colonies for the entire area.

Brunswick County began to function in 1732 and grew rapidly. The "overwrought ground" mentioned long before had in the interval became a more and more disturbing factor in agriculture. Tobacco was king, it demanded new land, hence new land must be provided. In Brunswick there was not only new land but the

Lancaster County Clerk's Office, Lancaster, Virginia

Essex County Clerk's Office, Tappahannock, Virginia

Richmond County Clerk's Office, Warsaw, Virginia

sort of land to raise good tobacco profitably, a condition equally true today. Settlers from Essex, King and Queen, Gloucester, York, Elizabeth City and other older counties soon made their way into Brunswick. It may not be amiss to observe that with the better living made possible by better tobacco crops a gastronomic delicacy was developed there, a rich and succulent stew called "Brunswick Stew" in honor of the county. So far as the writer is aware no other county in the state has achieved similar fame.

Orange County Reaches to the Mississippi

In 1734, an expansion to the northwest took place in the creation of Orange County so named to honor William, Prince of Orange, later William III of England. The City of Williamsburg, King William and King and Queen counties had been prior evidences of his popularity. The new division was to embrace that part of Spotsylvania County lying in Saint Mark's Parish "Bounden southerly by the line of Hanover County, northerly by the grant of Lord Fairfax and westerly by the utmost limits of Virginia." This western boundary was the Mississippi River. The Assembly further enacted "for the encouragement of the inhabitants already settled and which shall speedily settle on the westward of Sherrendo (Shenandoah) River" that "all who had established themselves by 1st January 1734/35 should be free of country, county and parish levies for the next three years."

Part of this expansion was due to the natural increase of population, the allure of new settlements where there was greater opportunity for advancement of fortunes, and part to the tide of immigration. Years of warfare in Germany had left ruined communities along the Rhenish Palatinate. For these people, Rotterdam was the most convenient port of embarkation and Philadelphia was often their port of debarkation. Following in the steps of John Van Metre, Adam Miller, Jacob Stover and Jost Hite who had come to the Valley of Virginia between 1725 and

23

1731, many immigrants, finding land cheaper in Virginia, left Pennsylvania and took up residence in Virginia.

In 1735, the act of the Assembly passed the year before for creating the new county of Amelia became effective. By this act, it was ordered that "the said county of Prince George and that part of the parish of Bristol which lies in the same be divided from the mouth of Namozain Creek up the same to the main, or John Hamlin's, fork of the said creek, thence up the south or lowest branch thereof to White Oak Hunting Path and thence by a south course to strike Nottoway River." The land below these courses retained the name of Prince George. The land lying above these courses bounded "southerly by the Great Nottoway River including part of the county of Brunswick and parish of Saint Andrew as far as to take the ridges between Roanoke and Appomattox Rivers and thence along those ridges to the great mountains westerly by the said mountains and northerly by the southern boundaries of Goochland and Henrico Counties" became Amelia County and Raleigh Parish. The name was in honor of the youngest daughter of George II.

By 1738, people living across the Blue Ridge Mountains found them a barrier to frequent attendance at Orange County Court. For their convenience, a division was ordered. "All that territory and tract of land at present deemed to be a part of the county of Orange lying on the northwest side of the said mountains (Blue Ridge) extending from thence northerly, westerly and southerly beyond the said mountains to the utmost limits of Virginia" shall be "separated from the rest of the said county and erected into two distinct counties and parishes; to be divided by a line to be run from the head spring of Hedgman River to the head spring by the River Potomac." "That part of the said territory lying to the northeast of the said line beyond the top of the said Blue Ridge shall be one distinct county, to be called and known by the name of the county of Frederick and parish of Frederick.

24

And that the rest of the said territory lying on the other side of the said line beyond the top of the said Blue Ridge shall be one other distinct county and parish to be called by the name of the county of Augusta and parish of Augusta." The counties thus created honored Frederick, Prince of Wales, eldest son of George II, and his wife, Augusta of Saxe-Gotha, Princess of Wales. Frederick predeceased his father and it was Frederick's son who became George III.

The Assembly had repeated with reference to Augusta and Frederick Counties its action in the case of Brunswick; namely: created counties before they were financially able to function. Not until 1743 did Frederick have sufficient tithables to begin to hold court, and it was two years later before Augusta set up her county organization.

In 1742, it was enacted that Prince William County be divided. The bounds of this county were set as follows: "all that part thereof lying on the south side of Occoquan and Bull Run and from the heads of the main branch of Bull Run by a straight course to the Thoroughfare of the Blue Ridge of Mountains known by the name of Ashby's Gap or Bent." Hamilton was the parish for Prince William County. That portion of Prince William which had, in 1732, been placed in Truro Parish became the new county of Fairfax. The name was, of course, in honor of Lord Fairfax, the Proprietor of the Northern Neck Grant.

Pohick, one of the churches in Truro Parish, is still standing and in use. General George Washington, who lived at nearby "Mount Vernon," George Mason of "Gunston Hall" and Lord Fairfax of "Greenway Court" were vestrymen; and planned for the erection of this present building in 1769.

In the same year that Fairfax was formed in the northern part of the colony, Hanover County in the middle section was divided. The Act ordered "all that tract of land now deemed to be a part of the said county of Hanover lying above a straight course to be run from the mouth of Little Rockey Creek on the River North-anna south, twenty degrees west until it intersects the line of Goochland County" should become a distinct county and known by the name of Louisa County. The name honored a daughter of George II, as Amelia had done a few years earlier.

Two years later the first of the eight counties eventually cut from Goochland was created and given the name Albemarle. This was in honor of William Anne Keppel, second Earl of Albemarle, Governor-General of the Colony, 1737-1754. Like most of the Governors-General, he did not come to Virginia, but the Lieutenant Governor as his deputy, performed the duties of his office.

The bounds of Albemarle were to be divided from Goochland on the west "by a line run from the point of fork of James River north, thirty degrees east to the Louisa County line, and from the said point of fork a direct course to Brooks mill and from thence the same course continued to Appomattox River." "The point of fork" is the junction of the Rivanna with the James. It will be noted by the reference to the Appomattox River that Albemarle extended across James River just as Goochland did. "Monticello" the beloved home of Thomas Jefferson, is in Albemarle County, and in architecture and planning is another example of the amazing versatility of his genius.

In 1746, the settlements in Brunswick County had grown to such an extent that a new division was required. The line was ordered "to be run from the county line where it crosses Roanoke River below the place called the Horse Ford to strike Nottoway River at the south." The territory above this line was to be called Lunenburg County. This title, anglicized from the German form, Luneburg, was chosen since the Duchy of Luneburg, like that of Brunswick, belonged to the Electorate of Hanover. Lunenburg embraced a vast acreage stretching from the rolling country where bright tobacco came to perfection as far west as the mountains and on the south to the North Carolina boundary.

26

CUMBERLAND, CULPEPER, SOUTHAMPTON AND CHESTERFIELD CREATED, 1749

The western portion of Goochland lying on both sides of the James had, in 1744, been taken to form the new county of Albemarle; now, five years later, the southeast portion of Goochland was made into the new county of Cumberland. The name was further honor for the Duke of Cumberland, "The Butcher of Culloden." The growth in this locality had been hastened by the arrival of numerous Huguenot families seeking asylum from persecution in France. Manakintown was the name of their settlement. The name is perpetuated in a newly erected Episcopal church not far from the site of the settlement where the Agee, Fourqurean, Legrand, Michaux, Guerrant, Flournoy and other families worship now, as they have done for some 250 years.

In the same year that Cumberland was formed, a new county was taken from Orange and named Culpeper, presumably in honor of Lord Culpeper, Governor of Virginia 1680-1683, a compliment to Lord Fairfax "who had inherited from him the ownership of the Northern Neck." Culpeper lay on the south side of the Rappahannock and north of the Conway River commonly called the fork of the Rappahannock River. The fork of the Rappahannock was the area between the Rappahannock River and its tributary, the Conway, now called the Rapidan. "Horsehoe Farm" is in Culpeper County and takes its name from the bend or horseshoe made by the Rapidan within which it is situated. While the residence is modern, the farm is of colonial times and was once owned by Governor Spotswood. It was from this house that, in 1741, he went to Annapolis, Maryland expecting to sail with an expedition to join Admiral Vernon and attack Cartagena in the Spanish Main. He died unexpectedly in Annapolis but, strangely enough, considering his prominence, his burial place is unknown.

Besides Culpeper and Cumberland, a third county, Southampton, was formed in 1749. This was taken from that portion of Isle of Wight's territory that lay west of Blackwater River. The name is said to honor, tho belatedly, Henry Wriothesley, second Earl of Southampton, friend of Shakespeare and a leading member of the Virginia Company of London. The City of Hampton and Hampton River honor the same person. Southampton is one of the cotton-raising counties of Virginia, and in the fall the fields of cotton are a beautiful sight.

Still a fourth county was formed in 1749 and that was Chesterfield. This, as was the case with the other three, represented no great expansion, but was in line with the thesis long before laid down—"to make justice accessible to all." Chesterfield is that part of Henrico that lay on the south side of James River. Again we go to England for the reason for this name and learn that it honors Philip Dormer Stanhope, fourth Earl of Chesterfield, the celebrated Lord Chesterfield. Though we think of him primarily as the epitome of good manners, courtesy and tact, his political career was important too. His services in Parliament, his lord lieutenancy of Ireland, his achievements on different embassies, and as Secretary of State were of value to his country. In Chesterfield County are the sites of the earliest iron works in the colony and of the projected college just beginning to operate when the 1622 Massacre destroyed everything.

In 1752, two new divisions were made. One of these was Halifax, the first of the nine counties that were destined to be carved out of the vast expanse of Lunenburg County. The bounds of Halifax were "all that part thereof lying on the south side of Black-Water Creek and Staunton river, from the said Black-Water creek to the confluence of the said river with the river Dan and from thence to Aaron's creek to the county line." The parish of Antrim coterminous with the county was established when the county was created. The name Halifax honors George Montagu Dunk, the second Earl of Halifax "who was First Lord of the Board of Trade about that time and as such greatly interested himself in the trade of the colonies." Halifax, Nova Scotia is a further memorial to Lord Halifax.

The other county created in 1752 was Dinwiddie, taken from the southern portion of Prince George. Its bounds began at the lower side "of the run which falls into Appomattox river between the town of Blanford and Bollings point warehouses to the outermost line of the glebe land and by a south course and by the said outermost line of the glebe land to Surry County." The name honored Robert Dinwiddie, Lieutenant Governor of Virginia 1751-58. He held office during the troubled period of the French and Indian Wars, in which George Washington, as a Colonel in the Virginia Militia, participated.

In 1754 that part of Amelia County divided "by a line to run from Ward's ford on Appomattox River to the mouth of Sail's creek on Nottoway river and all that part of the said county which lies on the upper side of the said line shall be one distinct county and called and known by the name of Prince Edward." The name was in honor of a younger brother of King George III, Prince Edward, Duke of Gloucester. This Prince was one of the two brothers of George III, whose marriages to commoners led to the passage of the famous Royal Marriage Act in 1772. Its well-known provisions are that no descendant of King George III may marry when under 25 years of age without consent of the reigning monarch or, if over that age, without a consenting Act of Parliament. Prince Edward Street in Fredericksburg is also named for this Prince as the city itself is for his father.

Also in 1754, a second county was created from Lunenburg and called Bedford. It comprised the area lying on the upper side of Falling-river from its mouth "up the said river to the fork, thence up that fork running by John Beard's to the head, thence by a line to be run from the head thereof north, twenty degrees east to the line dividing the said county from the county of Albemarle." It should be remembered that at this time both the present Buckingham and Appomattox were a part of Albemarle County. The new county honored "John Russell the fourth Duke of Bedford who was Secretary of State of Great Britain February 13th 1748 to June 26th 1757." The parish, coterminous with the county and created at the same time, also honored the Duke, being called Russell.

Another expansion at this time also on the south side of James River was the formation of Sussex from Surry County. Sussex lies to the south of Seacock Swamp on the line dividing Surry "from the county of Southampton, thence a straight course to Blackwater at the mouth of Coppohawk and up Blackwater to the line dividing" Surry from the county of Prince George. Sussex took its name from the English shire. Albemarle Parish formed in 1739 had included the area now made into Sussex, and, in addition, a small portion of Surry. It was enacted that the portion in Surry be added to Southwark Parish, and Albemarle Parish be made coterminous with Sussex.

The fourth county formed in 1754 was Hampshire named for the English shire. It is now in West Virginia. Since, however, its creation affected the bounds of two already established Virginia Counties, the Act of Assembly for its bounds is cited: "Whereas part of the county and parish of Augusta lies within the bounds of the territory or tract of land called the Northern Neck belong to the right honorable Thomas, Lord Fairfax, Baron of Cameron and it will be more convenient if the dividing line between the said territory and the other part of this colony be established as the line of the said county and that part of the said county be added to the county and parish of Frederick," it was enacted therefore that the part of Augusta above mentioned be added to Frederick which should then be divided into two counties and "all that part thereof lying to the westward of the ridge of mountains commonly called and known by the name of the Great North or Cape Capon mountains and Warin spring mountain extending to Potomac river be one distinct county and called and known by the name of Hampshire." When Augusta and Frederick were authorized in 1738, the western bounds of the Northern Neck Grant had not been surveyed. This was done in 1747, and the above Act changed the previous limits of Augusta so that the entire county would not be a part of the proprietary.

The name of the next new county reflected current happenings. For about six years, 1754-1760, the colony was actively participating in the struggle to crush French power in America. The Commander-in-Chief of the British Forces in America was, for a time, John Campbell, fourth Earl of Loudoun. His conduct of the war was severely criticized, and he was recalled in December 1757. He was, for almost two years, titular "Governor and Captain-General of Virginia," though his deputy Lieutenant-Governor Robert Dinwiddie performed all the duties of the office. Loudoun, the new county named for the Earl, was formed from Fairfax County in 1757. It included "all that part thereof lying above Difficult Run which falls into Potomac river and by a line to be run from the head of the said run or straight course to the mouth of Rocky run." The part "thereof below the said run and course" retained its status as a distinct county and the name of Fairfax.

In 1759, the inhabitants of Prince William County complained of many inconveniences "by reason of the great extent thereof and their remote situation from the courthouse." Mindful that justice be accessible to all, the Assembly enacted that Prince William be divided and "all that part of the said county that lies above a line to be run from the head of Bull Run and along the top of Bull run mountains to Chapman's mill, in Broad run thoroughfare, from thence by a direct line till it intersects the nearest part of the line dividing Stafford and Prince William Counties" be known as Fauquier. This again honors an English official but in this case a very popular one, Francis Fauquier, who, in 1758, succeeded Robert Dinwiddie as Lieutenant Governor of Virginia. He served the colony for nearly ten years, dying in Williamsburg on 3 March 1768 "after a tedious illness which he bore with the greatest patience and fortitude." Among the eulogies in prose to his memory, the following verse may be noted:

"If ever virtue lost a friend sincere
If ever sorrow claimed Virginia's tear
If ever death a noble conquest made
'Twas when Fauquier the debt of nature paid"

With tobacco as the medium of exchange and as the most valuable export, the economic base was too small for the large superstructure erected on it. The taxes, fees, and commissions on exported tobacco were numerous and onerous, the net return to the planter often did not cover the goods he had ordered and his debt to his London agent increased. It was British policy that her colonies should send her raw materials and buy from her manufactured articles, thus giving her merchants a double advantage and placing the colonists at double disadvantage. During the 1750's, the colony had been put to such great expense in prosecuting the French and Indian War that for the first time an issue of paper money was required. Economic conditions grew worse throughout the colony.

"WESTWARD-HO" TWENTY-SIX NEW COUNTIES, 1750-1770

The unceasing westward trek of settlers continued. In 1750-60, eight counties were formed, between 1760-1770, eighteen new divisions occurred, which evidences the great growth of population.

Albemarle was the next county to be divided. In 1761, it was enacted that the portion "of the said county which lies on the south side of the Fluvanna river" [old name for the James River above Richmond] "shall be one distinct county and called and known by the name of Buckingham." By the same legislation, "that other part of the said county which lies on the north side of the Fluvanna river shall be divided from the confluence of

32

Rockfish river with the Fluvanna by Rockfish river to the mouth of Green creek and thence a straight line to the house of Thomas Bell to the Blue mountains, and all that part which lies above Rockfish river and the lines aforesaid" shall be called Amherst County. Amherst Parish at the same time was formed from Saint Anne's Parish and made coterminous with the county of Amherst. Several years earlier, Tillotson Parish had been formed from Saint Anne's to take care of the residents of Amherst who lived on the south side of James River. It was now made coterminous with the county of Buckingham.

The name Buckingham is probably for the Duke of Buckingham. Amherst derives its name from "the hero of Ticonderoga, Major-General Sir Jeffrey Amherst, the most successful as well as the most popular of all the English Colonial Governors-General." He was titular Governor-General of Virginia 1759-1768 while Francis Fauquier performed the duties of the office.

Four years passed, and two more divisions were made in the western portion of Lunenburg. The part of Lunenburg comprised in the parish of Cornwall became Charlotte County and the portion in the parish of St. James became Mecklenburg.

These counties were named, as is the city of Charlottesville, after Charlotte of Mecklenburg-Strelitz, who became Queen of England on her marriage to King George III.

We next find in 1767 that Halifax has grown to the point of division and a new county, Pittsylvania, has been taken from its western portion. Pittsylvania lay on the upper or western side "of a line to be run across the mouth of Strait Stone creek on Staunton river to the country line, near the mouth of the country line creek on Dan river." At the same time, Antrim, which was the parish for Halifax, was divided and the part lying in Pittsylvania became Camden. Pittsylvania honored "Sir William Pitt, Earl of Chatham, the celebrated English statesman" whose sympathy with them had endeared him to the colonists. A statue of him in Westmoreland county, Virginia and another in Charleston, South Carolina are further expressions of the affection felt for him.

Botetourt, 1770 Honors a Popular Colonial Governor

The next county was, in the main, a rearrangement of already settled territory bearing always in mind that easy access to justice was the purpose of every division. The new county, Botetourt, was formed from Augusta in 1770 and lay on the south side of a dividing "line beginning at the Blue Ridge, running north fifty-five degrees west, to the confluence of Mary's creek, or the south river, with the north branch of James River, thence up the same to the mouth of Carr's creek, thence up the said creek to the mountain, thence north, fifty-five degrees west as far as the courts of the two counties shall extend it." The phrase to note in the above is: "as far as the courts of the two counties shall extend it," in other words, there was no limit to the western boundary. The name Botetourt was for Norborne Berkeley, Lord de Botetourt, Governor of Virginia 1768-1770. He died in Williamsburg in October 1770, lamented and beloved for his interest in the colony and the College of William and Mary. The House of Burgesses voted a sum of money to have a statue of him made in London to stand in the old Capitol building. The statue still exists, one of the most treasured possessions of the College of William and Mary, and adorns its campus.

Frederick Subdivided

Two years later, the county of Frederick had a division on both its eastern and northern ends. It was enacted by the Assembly that the territory of Frederick be divided into three distinct counties: "on the north by a line beginning in the line that divides the counties of Frederick and Loudoun one mile and an half northward of the corner in Williams' gap that at present divides the parishes of Frederick and Norborne thence westward with a line exactly parallel to the line that now divides the said parishes of Frederick and Norborne till it intersects the line of Hampshire county; thence with the Hampshire line to the corner dividing the parishes of Frederick and Beckford; thence with the lines dividing the said parishes of Frederick and Beckford east southeast to the south eastwardly bank of Cedar creek, thence binding on the same to its confluence with the river Shenandoah; thence across the said river east to the easterly bank of the same; thence down the said river and binding on the same to the mouth of Passage creek; and thence with a right line to the line of Culpeper, at the intersection of the road leading through Chester's gap; thence with the Culpeper, Fauquier, and Loudoun lines to the beginning." This area, so described, was to remain Frederick County. "All that part of the county which lies between the first mentioned line running from the said beginning in the line of Loudoun county and Potomac river shall be . . . known by the name of Berkeley county." The remainder of what had been Frederick now became Dunmore County. There had been three parishes in Frederick; of these Frederick remained in the county, while Norborne appropriately became the parish for Berkeley and Beckford for Dunmore.

Berkeley County named for Norborne Berkeley, Lord de Botetourt, later became a part of West Virginia. It was further evidence of this governor's popularity, Botetourt County having previously been named for him.

Dunmore Renamed Shenandoah

Dunmore honored the new Governor, John Murray, Earl of Dunmore, who succeeded Lord Botetourt. His popularity was short lived, and his tyrannical acts, when he attempted to keep the colony loyal to the crown, so enraged the people that he was forced to take refuge with his family on a British warship. In 1777, still smarting over his behavior, the Assembly changed the name of the county to Shenandoah for the beautiful river that flows through it; the change to take effect February 1, 1778.

Fincastle Reaches to the Ohio River

In 1772, the county of Fincastle was formed from the western portion of Botetourt. It is an evidence of rapidly growing settlements when for the first time mention is made of "inhabitants and settlers on the waters of Holston and New rivers." The territory of Fincastle was "within a line to run up the east side of New river to the mouth of Culberson's creek, thence a direct line to the Catawba road where it crosses the dividing ridge between the north fork of Roanoke and the waters of New river, thence with the top of the ridge to the bent where it turns eastwardly, thence a south course crossing Little river to the top of the Blue Ridge of mountains." The reason for the name Fincastle seems uncertain; one version has it as being for George, Lord Fincastle, Lord Dunmore's son, and the other that it was for the town of Fincastle established in 1772 and so named for Lord Botetourt's home in England.

Virginia Counties Extended to the Ohio River and Include Kentucky

Fincastle County was an expansion of Augusta to the west but an expansion to the northwest had been in progress since before 1754. In that year, Governor Dinwiddie ordered a fort built on the present site of Pittsburgh and issued a proclamation offering land in the area to those who would enlist as soldiers for the French and Indian War. The French captured the fort and named it Fort Duquesne. This outpost of great strategic importance fell to the English in 1758 and was renamed Fort Pitt. The area was under Virginia jurisdiction and called the district of West Augusta being considered a part of Augusta County. "County courts were held at Pittsburgh under Virginia jurisdiction and the great section of country from the Alleghany mountains northwest to the Ohio came to be called West Augusta. It was represented under this name in the Conventions of

1775 and 1776. In October 1776, the district of West Augusta was divided into the counties of Ohio, Yohogania and Monongalia. A portion of this territory, including Pittsburgh, was claimed by Pennsylvania and there was much disorder and some bloodshed between the officers and adherents of the two Colonies. In 1779, commissioners from Virginia and Pennsylvania finally settled the line and Pittsburgh and the adjoining area were surrendered to Pennsylvania." The above is the concise account, by the late W. G. Stanard, in an early volume of the *Virginia Magazine of History and Biography,* of an almost forgotten episode in western development. It explains why in the Augusta County records in Staunton, Virginia are found deeds for land now in Pennsylvania.

The bounds of these three new counties, Ohio, Yohogania and Monongalia are set forth in detail in the Act of Assembly creating them, but are not quoted here since they neither adjoin nor are a part of the Commonwealth of Virginia now.

Kentucky a Virginia County, 1776

The next division of a county occurred in this same year 1776, and was further expansion toward the beckoning west; this division was not to take effect until January first, 1777. Fincastle became extinct as a county, its territory becoming Kentucky, Washington and Montgomery Counties. The Act of Assembly recites that the part of Fincastle lying "to the south and westward of a line beginning on the Ohio at the mouth of Great Sandy creek and running up the same and the main, or northeasterly, branch thereof to the Great Laurel Ridge or Cumberland Mountain, thence south westerly along the said mountain to the line of North Carolina shall be one distinct county and called and known by the name of Kentucky; and all that part of the said county of Fincastle included in the lines beginning at the Cumberland Mountain where the line of Kentucky county intersects the North Carolina line, thence east along the said

Carolina line to the top of Iron mountain, thence along the same easterly to the source of the south fork of Holstein river, thence northwardly along the highest part of the high lands, ridges and mountains that divide the waters of the Tennessee from those of the Great Kanawha, to the most easterly source of Clinch river, thence westwardly along the top of the mountains that divide the waters of Clinch river from those of the Great Kanawha and Sandy Creek to the line of Kentucky county thence along the same to the beginning" shall be known "by the name of Washington; and all the residue of the said county of Fincastle shall be" known as Montgomery.

It is said that Washington County is the first place or area named for General Washington in the United States. It is also the first time the words Kentucky and Tennessee occur in a county division and show the scope of western settlements. Montgomery County was named for General Richard Montgomery, a Revolutionary officer, who fell 31 December 1775, while trying unsuccessfully to scale the city walls and capture Quebec from the English.

The next formation was a division of Pittsylvania County in 1777, ten years after its creation. The new county lay on the west side of "a line beginning at the mouth of Blackwater on Staunton river and running parallel with the line of Halifax county till it strikes the country line." The name Henry honored Patrick Henry, the famous orator of the Revolution and first Governor of the Commonwealth of Virginia. He purchased a large acreage in Henry County but resided in nearby Campbell County.

Also, in 1777, Albemarle was divided "by a line beginning at the most western point in the line of Louisa County and running thence directly to the lower edge of Stott's ferry on the Fluvanna river and that part which lies south eastward of the said line together with the islands in the Fluvanna river adjacent thereto shall be called by the name of Fluvanna county." The county was named for the river and the river was so called in honor of Queen Anne whose name is borne by four other Virginia rivers. Fluvanna, used for most of the eighteenth century, was the title given the James River above its falls at Richmond. Tobacco and other merchandise was taken in bateaux down this river to Richmond.

Both Henry and Fluvanna Counties had been formed mostly because of natural increase in population rather than of any tide of immigration. The creation of Powhatan County in 1777 was of the same type. This county embraced the portion of Cumberland lying on the south side of James River and in Southam Parish, which was the eastern end of Cumberland and adjoined Chesterfield County. The name Powhatan honored the celebrated Indian chieftain.

In 1778, the vast sprawling territory of Augusta underwent changes. One was an addition to Hampshire County of the territory on the north of "a line beginning at the north side of the North Mountain opposite to the upper end of Sweedland Hill and running a direct course so as to strike the mouth of Seneca creek on the north fork of the south branch of Potomac river and the same course to be continued to the Allegheny mountain, thence along the said mountain" to the county line. "The residue of the county and parish of Augusta" was divided by a line beginning "at the South Mountain and running thence by Benjamin Yardley's plantation so as to strike the north river below James Byrd's house thence up the said river to the mouth of Naked creek, thence leaving the river a direct course so as to cross the said river at the mouth of Cunningham's branch in the upper end of Silas Hart's land to the foot of North Mountain, thence fifty-five degrees west to the Allegheny mountain and with the same to the line of Hampshire"; all the portion north eastward of this line was to be called Rockingham. It is supposed the name of this county honors the Marquis of Rockingham, Prime Minister of England in 1765-66 when the unpopular Stamp Act was repealed.

In the same Act of Assembly, 1778, by which Rockingham was created Greenbrier County, now in West Virginia, was formed from Montgomery and Botetourt Counties to the west of "a line beginning on the top of the ridge which divides the Eastern from the Western Waters, where the line between Augusta and Botetourt crosses the same, and running thence the same course continued north fifty-five degrees west to the Ohio, thence beginning at the said ridge at the said lines of Botetourt and Augusta, running along the top of the said ridge, passing the Sweet Springs to the top of Peter's mountain, thence along the said mountain to the line of Montgomery county, thence along the same mountain to the Kanawha or New river, thence down the said river to the Ohio." Greenbrier County takes its name from its principal river. It is the anglicized version of the French word "ronce" for brier or bramble and "verte" for green. The town Ronceverte, situated on the river, keeps the French word.

At the same time Rockbridge County was formed from parts of Botetourt and Augusta. It was bounded "by a line beginning in the top of the Blue Ridge near Steele's mill and running thence north fifty-five degrees west passing the said mill and crossing the North mountain to the top and the mountain dividing the waters of the Calf Pasture from the waters of the Cow Pasture and thence along the said mountain crossing Panther's gap to the line that divides the counties of Augusta and Botetourt." The remainder of Botetourt shall be divided "by a line to begin at Audley Paul's and running thence south fifty-five degrees east crossing James river, to the top of the Blue Ridge, thence along the same crossing James river, to the beginning of the aforesaid line dividing Augusta county; then beginning again at the said Audley Paul's, and running north fifty-five degrees west till the said course shall intersect a line to be run south

40

forty-five degrees west from the place where the above line dividing Augusta terminated."

The enabling acts setting forth the bounds for the counties when created have been quoted fully, both for the information they contain and for the comprehensive geographical knowledge they reveal. They show painstaking surveys and study to achieve accuracy under the handicap of lack of roads and bridges. In addition to technical knowledge, the surveyor needed a sturdy physique to withstand the daily hardships that were part of his routine work.

Rockbridge, the name of the new county whose bounds have been described, commemorated the unique scenic wonder within its confines known as Natural Bridge. This is a span of stone 215 feet high over Cedar Creek. Once a trail passed over it and now a modern highway. It has been known and visited since 1770.

West of the Ohio and to the Mississippi. Illinois County Formed

Illinois, the last county to be formed in the decade 1770 to 1780 was an area on the western side of the Ohio River which had been a part of Augusta County. In the preamble to the Act creating this county, the Assembly noted with satisfaction that "by a sucessful expedition carried on by the Virginia militia on the western side of the Ohio river several of the British posts within the territory of this commonwealth in the country adjacent to the river Mississippi have been reduced." This, of course, was a reference to George Rogers Clark whose exploits secured the Mississippi Valley area for Virginia and the United States. Illinois County was a part of the large territory given by Virginia to the nation in 1783.

Kentucky County Divided

The next event was the division of the unwieldly county of Kentucky into three parts; Jefferson, Fayette and Lincoln, with the towns of Louisville, Lexington and Harrodsburg for their respective county seats. Jefferson County was so named to honor Thomas Jefferson, and was the first honor of this sort accorded him. Fayette was for the beloved ally, the Marquis de la Fayette and Lincoln for General Benjamin Lincoln of the Revolution. When compelled to surrender Charleston, South Carolina to the British, he had endured the humiliation of giving up his sword to Sir Henry Clinton. In return, when Yorktown was captured and Lord Cornwallis required to yield his sword, General Lincoln was awarded the distinction of receiving it. Cornwallis, however, did not appear in person, and it was his aide who handed the sword to General Lincoln. From these three counties was formed the present Commonwealth of Kentucky.

A division of Brunswick in the south eastern part of the state took place now and Greensville County came into being. This lay to the east of a line beginning "two miles above Chapman's ford on Meherrin river and running a due south course to the boundary line between this state and North Carolina and from the station aforesaid by another line due north to Nottoway river." The name selected for this county commemorated General Nathanael Greene of the Revolution who marched into this area on his return from the Battle of Guilford Court House.

In 1782, occurred a division of Bedford County. The eastern end was cut from the whole and named for General William Campbell, the hero of King's Mountain, one of the decisive battles of the Revolution. Campbell lies to the east of a line beginning "at the mouth of Judy's creek on James river, thence to Thompson's mill on Buffalo creek, thence to the mouth of Back creek on Goose creek thence the same course continued to Staunton river." Staunton is the name given the Roanoke River as it passes through Bedford, Campbell, Charlotte and Halifax Counties. In Mecklenburg, it resumes its original name of Roanoke and so continues into Albemarle Sound.

The next development was Harrison, taken from Monongalia

County. Neither is now a Virginia county, but it is mentioned since it honors Benjamin Harrison, one of the seven Virginia Signers of the Declaration of Independence who also completed in 1784, the year the county was formed, a three year term as Governor of the Commonwealth.

In the next year, a new county, Nelson, now in Kentucky, was created. This, too, honored a former Governor and Signer of the Declaration of Independence, Thomas Nelson. It was his home in Yorktown that Lord Cornwallis used as his headquarters during the siege and battle.

In 1786, Franklin was formed out of "that part of the county of Bedford lying south of Staunton river together with so much of the county of Henry lying north of a line to be run from the head of Shooting creek to the west end of Turkeycock mountain, thence along the top of the mountain to intersect the dividing line between the counties of Henry and Pittsylvania, thence along that line to the mouth of Blackwater river." The reason for this name is obvious: all America honored the achievements of Benjamin Franklin.

Deed of Cession. Virginia Gives the Northwest Territory

The tempo of western expansion had increased to such an extent that four counties were formed in 1786. One of these, Hardy, lies now in West Virginia as does its parent county of Hampshire. It might be well to explain now, even though out of chronological sequence, the genesis of West Virginia. In May 1861 when Governor Letcher called out the Virginia militia, many persons living beyond the Alleghanies throughout that section of Virginia bordering on Ohio and Pennsylvania were not in sympathy with his action. The residents of some forty counties held a convention and were almost unanimous in their desire to break away from Virginia and form a new state. A constitution was framed which was ratified by the people in May 1862. The following year, 1863, West Virginia became a state of the Union

43

and at one blow, Virginia lost a third of her territory. The loss of the rich coal fields and other natural resources of West Virginia impoverished the Old Dominion more severely and made "Reconstruction Days" longer and more difficult than they might otherwise have been.

Returning to Hardy County, we learn that it was named for Samuel Hardy formerly of Isle of Wight County "one of the number who signed the Deed of Cession which transferred the Northwest Territory to the General Government."

Virginia's claim to territory was of long standing, her charters of 1609 and 1612 giving her dominion to the Pacific Ocean, but no exploration beyond the Mississippi had been attempted. Her claim of dominion to the Mississippi, however, was of more substantial character. In 1778 with a picked force of 180 Virginia riflemen, George Rogers Clark captured the great Northwest Territory from the English "in one of the most amazing exploits in American history." This territory Virginia organized as "the county of Illinois." "But for Clark's conquest the treaty of 1783 might well have fixed the nation's western boundary at the Alleghanies instead of at the Mississippi." Almost all the Ohio Valley and parts of Wisconsin and Michigan were included in this voluntary gift that Virginia made in 1783 to the weak confederated colonies. In 1785 Congress passed a Land Ordinance providing for the sale of this land. "Thus this cession provided the infant republic with its only sure source of revenue" since at that time "Congress had neither the power to impose nor the machinery to collect any taxes."

The other three counties formed in 1786 lie now in Kentucky which, in 1792, was "organized as a state out of Virginia territory with her consent." These divisions are Mercer and Madison, created out of Lincoln, and Bourbon out of Fayette. Mercer honored General Hugh Mercer of the Revolution; Madison, James Madison, later known as the "Father of the Constitution,"

44

and Bourbon, the French reigning family, particularly Louis XVI who had given aid in the Revolution.

The next county, Russell, was taken from Washington. Its bounds are: "all that part of the said county lying within a line to be run along the Clinch mountain to the Carolina line; thence with that line to the Cumberland mountain, and the extent of country between the Cumberland mountain, Clinch mountain and the line of Montgomery county shall be one distinct county and called and known by the name of Russell." The name was selected as a tribute to General William Russell "who distinguished himself at the Battle of King's mountain." Russell remains a Virginia county.

Five westward expansions now occur in quick succession. In 1787, from Harrison was formed Randolph County named for Edmund Randolph, first Attorney General of the Commonwealth and a member of the Continental Congress. Both Harrison and Randolph are in West Virginia. Pendleton, also now in West Virginia, was formed in 1788 from portions of Hardy, Augusta, and Rockingham counties. It is named for Edmund Pendleton, President of the Virginia Convention of 1775.

The next year two new Kentucky counties were formed; Mason from Bourbon and Woodford from Fayette. The former took its name from George Mason of "Gunston Hall," author of the Bill of Rights and the latter from General William Woodford, a native of Caroline County, Virginia who rendered distinguished service in the Revolution and later moved to Kentucky.

At the same time, a new county destined to be in West Virginia was formed from Greenbrier and part of Montgomery counties and given the name of Kanawha from the river.

The only one of the counties formed in 1789 that is now in Virginia is Nottoway. This was comprised of that part of Amelia County "lying south of a line to begin at a place called Wells bridge on Namozene creek which divides the said county from the county of Dinwiddie, thence running through the said county of Amelia so as to strike the line of Prince Edward county five miles west of a place called Ward's ford on Appomattox river." Nottoway is an Indian word meaning "a snake, that is, an enemy." Nottoway River derives its name from the Indian tribe and the county honors both.

1790-1800 EXPANSION IN THE FIRST DECADE AFTER THE REVOLUTION

The next year a county was cut from Montgomery and named Wythe. It lies to the "south-west of a line beginning on the Henry line at the head of Big Reedy Island, from thence to the waggon ford on Peck creek, thence to the clover bottom on Blue Stone, thence to the Kanawha county line." The name is for George Wythe, eminent jurist and a Signer of the Declaration of Independence. Elected in 1779 to the Chair of Law and Police, recently established at the College of William and Mary, he "became the first occupant of a chair of law in America, and the second in the English speaking world." The first chair of law established in England was at Oxford University, and Sir William Blackstone was the first professor.

The year 1791 saw the formation of three counties, all of them rearrangement of lines in established communities rather than expansion into new territory. The first was the division of Henry into two counties: "all that part of the said county lying west of a line beginning on the line dividing the counties of Henry and Franklin one mile above where it crosses Town creek, a branch of Smith's river, thence a parallel line with Pittsylvania line to the country line shall be one distinct county and called and known by the name of Patrick." The name, of course, was the given name of the great orator, and since Henry County bore his surname, the new division took his given name. It is a county of beautiful mountains with panoramic views. The Fairy Stone State Park is within its borders. On Fairy Stone

46

Mountain and in the streams at its base are found tiny stones shaped like crosses. The story is that the gentle fairy folk when they heard of our Lord's Crucifixion wept profusely and their tears turned to stone crosses as they fell, a lasting memorial of their grief.

The next county, formed in 1791, was Bath. Its bounds are thus described: "All those parts of the counties of Augusta, Botetourt and Greenbrier within the following bounds, to wit: beginning at the west corner of Pendleton county, thence to the top of the ridge dividing the headwaters of the South branch from those of Jackson's river, thence a straight line to the lower end of John Redman's plantation on the Cowpasture river, thence to the top of the ridge that divides the waters of the Cow-pasture from those of the Calf-pasture thence along the same as far as the ridge that divides Hamilton's creek from Mill creek, thence to the Mill mountain, and with the same to the north corner of the line of Rockbridge county, thence along the said mountain crossing the line of Botetourt county to the ridge that divides the waters of Pad's creek from those of Simpson's creek, thence along the said ridge to the Cow-pasture river, thence crossing the said river a direct course and crossing Jackson's river at the mouth of Dunlap's creek, thence up the same as far as the narrows above the plantation of David Tate, Senr., so as to leave the inhabitants of the said creek in Botetourt county, thence a direct course to the top of the Allegany mountain where the road from the Warm Springs to Greenbrier court house crosses the said mountain, thence along the top of the said mountain opposite the headwaters of Anthony's creek, thence a direct course crossing Greenbrier river to the end of the Droop mountain, thence up the same to the great Greenbrier mountain thence along the said mountain to the line of Randolph county thence with the same along the said mountain dividing the waters of Monongalia and Cheat from those of Greenbrier river, and thence to its beginning shall form one distinct county."

47

The above is quoted in full since the names used are still in use, and it is possible to judge from them the extent of the county. Warm Springs is still in Bath, but Narrows is in Giles County, and Alleghany County lies between Bath and Giles.

The name Bath derives from the medical springs within its boundaries, which for many years during the summer months were visited by persons from as far south as Louisiana. Families drove up in their carriages and stayed for months to enjoy the curative effects of the waters and bracing mountain air.

The third county formed in 1791 was Mathews which was taken from Gloucester. It lies "to the eastward of a line to begin at the mouth of North river, thence up the meanders thereof to the mill, thence up the eastern branch of the millpond to the head of Muddy creek thence down the said creek to Pianka-tank river." The name is said to be in honor of a Major Thomas Mathews of the Revolution who afterwards was prominent in the legislature representing the Borough of Norfolk in the House of Delegates from 1785 to 1791.

In 1793, there were also three counties formed. One of these, Grayson, was taken from Wythe as follows: "Beginning in the Washington line where it joins the Iron Mountain, thence along the said mountain to a spur of the same that forms Ewing mountain, keeping the ridge that divides the waters of Cripple and Bush creeks to the top of the said mountain, thence a straight course to the Popular Camp mountain by Rose's mill thence to the mouth of Greasy creek thence a straight course to the Montgomery line." Grayson took its name from Colonel William Grayson, an officer in the Revolution, member of the Continental Congress and one of the first two senators elected from Virginia after the adoption of the Constitution to serve in the Congress of the United States. Unfortunately his tenure of office was short; he died 12 March 1790.

Also in 1793, Russell County was divided and all that part "which lies westwardly of a line beginning on the top of Clinch mountain, one mile eastwardly of big Maukason gap, thence a direct course to the mouth of Stock creek thence up the same to Powell's mountain, thence due north to the Kentucky boundary shall form one distinct county and be called and known by the name of Lee." The name honored General Henry Lee who was Governor of Virginia 1791-1794. He is more often called "Light Horse Harry Lee" from the fact that he commanded, during the Revolution, light horse cavalry. He was the father of General Robert E. Lee. Lee is the county farthest to the west and adjoins Tennessee and Kentucky.

Also in 1793, the county of Madison was formed from Culpeper. Its bounds were within a line "Beginning at the mouth of Robinson river thence up the same to the mouth of Crooked run, thence up the said run to the mountain road where Tennant's church formerly stood, thence a straight course to the head of Hugh's river in the Blue Ridge, thence the same course continued to the top of the ridge and to the line of Shenandoah county, thence westwardly on the top of the ridge with the lines of the counties of Shenandoah and Rockingham to the line of Orange county to the beginning." One may wonder that the name Madison was used again, but at this date the earlier Madison County lay in Kentucky. When in 1792 Kentucky achieved statehood, it was composed of nine counties formerly in Virginia; namely: Fayette, Lincoln, Jefferson, Madison, Mercer, Nelson, Bourbon, Mason and Woodford.

Four years after Madison County, Virginia was formed, Brooke was cut from Ohio County. This name was for Robert Brooke, Governor of Virginia 1794 to 1796. He was a grandson of the Robert Brooke who, in 1716, accompanied Governor Spotswood on the famous expedition across the Blue Ridge Mountains. Both Brooke and Ohio are now in West Virginia.

In 1798, Wood was established from Harrison County. It is named for James Wood, Governor of Virginia 1796 to 1799, and son of Colonel James Wood, an early settler in the Valley of

49

Virginia, and founder of the city of Winchester. Wood and Harrison are also West Virginia counties.

The next county created, also destined to lie in West Virginia, was Monroe. This was formed from Greenbrier County and named to honor James Monroe. Born, like General Washington, in Westmoreland County, he had a long political career culminating in the Presidency of the United States. The creed he expounded, called the "Monroe Doctrine", is still followed by our government.

THE NEW CENTURY BRINGS SIX NEW COUNTIES 1800-1810

As the new century, 1800, came in, Tazewell was formed from Wythe and Russell counties. Its bounds were all that part of the aforesaid counties "beginning on the Kanawha line and running with the line which divides Montgomery and Wythe counties to where the said line crosses the top of Brushy mountain, thence along the top of the said mountain to its junction with the Garden mountain, thence along the top of the said mountain to the Clinch mountain, thence along the top of the said mountain to the head of Cove creek, a branch of the Maiden Spring fork of Clinch river; thence a straight line to Mann's gap in Kent's ridge; thence north forty-five degrees west, to the line which divides the state of Kentucky from that of Virginia; thence along said line to the Kanawha line and with said line to the place of beginning." The name honored Henry Tazewell, United States senator from Virginia 1794-1799.

In 1801, Virginia made a second attempt to honor Thomas Jefferson by naming the new county taken from Berkeley in his honor. The Jefferson County formed in 1780 was, in 1801, a part of Kentucky and this new county was destined to fall in West Virginia; hence no county within the present confines of the state honors this great Virginian.

Harper's Ferry, situated in Jefferson County at the confluence of the Shenandoah with the Potomac River, is as well known for the beauty of its location as for being the site of John Brown's Raid, the prelude to civil warfare. Incidentally it may be noted that the Shenandoah afforded an outlet to market for the produce of the Valley of Virginia since boats could pass down its waters into the Potomac and thus to Chesapeake Bay.

In 1804, the new county of Mason was formed from Kanawha. It was bounded as follows: "beginning at the mouth of Little Guyandotte River running from thence to the northwest corner of a survey of 1437½ acres made for Thomas Lewis in Teaze's valley near the house of Joshua Morris, from thence to the mouth of Little Hurricane creek, thence crossing the Kanawha river and taking a dividing ridge between Eighteen Mile and Pocatallico creeks to the end thereof, thence pursuing a northeast direction till it intersects the Wood County line to the Ohio, thence down the Ohio to the beginning."

Within this county lies Point Pleasant, scene of the famous battle.

This was the second time that Virginia had attempted to pay honor to George Mason of "Gunston Hall", author of the Bill of Rights. The earlier Mason County formed in 1789 became a part of Kentucky three years later, and the later Mason was destined to lie in West Virginia. George Mason, Thomas Jefferson and the Marquis de la Fayette are not represented in the list of Virginia counties.

The county of Giles formed in 1806 was created from portions of Montgomery, Monroe and Tazewell counties, and is now a border county between Virginia and West Virginia. Its boundaries are thus described: "Beginning at the end of Gauley mountain on New River, where the counties of Greenbrier and Kanawha intersect, thence up the river with the Greenbrier and Montgomery lines to the intersection of Monroe line; thence with the Monroe and Montgomery line to the upper end of Pine's plantation; thence a straight line to the mouth of Rich creek, leaving the plantation of Hugh Caperton on the right; thence with the Mon-

51

roe line to the intersection of Botetourt County line and with the Botetourt and Montgomery lines to the top of Gap mountain; thence along the top of the said mountain to New River crossing the same to the end of Walker's creek mountain; thence along the top of the said mountain to the intersection of Wythe county line; thence northwestwardly with said line to the intersection of Tazewell line, and with the Tazewell and Montgomery line to the top of Wolf creek mountain; thence along Wolf creek mountain to a path leading from the Round Bottom to Harman's mill about three miles below the mouth of Clear Fork of Wolf creek; thence a straight line to the mouth of Militin's fork; thence a direct line to the head of Crane creek on the top of the Flat-top mountain; thence a direct line to the three forks of Guyandotte river; thence down said river until it intersects Kanawha county line; thence with said line to the beginning."

Mountain Lake is situated in Giles County, and is a well-known summer resort. It is also of interest for the wide range of plant life found in its vicinity. Members of the University of Virginia's Biological Department maintain a field station there and in the summer study the wide variety of plants growing nearby.

Giles County was named in honor of William B. Giles who in 1800 was prominent in Virginia politics. He later served as Governor 1827-1830.

In 1808 Amherst County was divided according to its parish lines, the western or upper part of the county which lay in Lexington Parish retained the name of Amherst, and the lower or more eastern part took the name of Nelson. This as will be recalled was the second attempt to honor Governor Thomas Nelson, whose Yorktown home still holds buried in its eastern wall two cannon balls, grim mementoes of the battle of Yorktown.

Virginia has believed in honoring the men who have held the gubernatorial office, nineteen having been thus commemorated, and Cabell County formed in 1809 carried on the tradition. It honored William H. Cabell, who served from 1805 until 1808 when he was chosen judge of the General Court. It later fell into West Virginia, and lies along the Ohio River.

1810-1820, DEVELOPMENT CONTINUES, FIVE NEW COUNTIES

In 1814, a Virginia county was formed from parts of Lee, Russell and Washington and named Scott. This name was selected because of General Winfield Scott, a native of Virginia who achieved fame because of his successes in the War of 1812. Later in the Mexican War he decisively defeated the Mexicans at Chapultepec, entering Mexico City as conqueror. As a result of this war some 850,000 square miles became United States territory.

The bounds of Scott County are as follows: "Beginning at the head of Reedy creek where the wagon road crosses the same in the county of Washington thence down the Tennessee line to the south fork of Clinch river thence northward passing the Flag Pond to the top of Powell's mountain in Lee County and along it to the county of Russell and with it to the Kentucky line, thence along Cumberland mountain to the head of Guese's river thence down the Clinch mountain thence to the western end of Samuel Hensley's plantation and thence to the beginning."

"The wagon road" mentioned in the above description is most likely the so-called "Wilderness Road" over which many west bound settlers laboriously toiled. The other route west that was often used was north to the present Pittsburgh and down the Ohio river. Powell's Mountain and the river of that name commemorate Ambrose Powell of Culpeper County, one of the earliest explorers of Kentucky who accompanied Doctor Thomas Walker there in 1749. In Scott County is the Natural Tunnel, a rare formation through which the trains of the Southern Railway Company pass regularly en route to Tennessee.

Tyler, the next county established, lies now in the northwestern part of West Virginia along the Ohio River but commemorates a Tidewater Virginian, John Tyler, Sr. He was born at

53

"Greenway" Charles City County and served as Governor 1808-1811. His fame has been somewhat obscured by that of his son, John Tyler, junior, President of the United States.

The next county formed, Lewis, which was cut from Harrison, also lay later in West Virginia in the north central area. It derived its name from a heroic soldier, Colonel Charles Lewis who was killed at the Battle of Point Pleasant in 1774. Point Pleasant, situated near the confluence of the Great Kanawha with the Ohio River was the scene of a day-long bloody battle between the Virginia troops and Indian warriors led by Cornstalk and Logan. General Andrew Lewis, brother of Colonel Charles, was the commanding officer. The battle was hardly decisive and General Lewis wished to follow and annihilate the fleeing enemy. Lord Dunmore, in command of another detachment which arrived later, forbade this and allowed the Indians to escape. This may have been one of the reasons that influenced the Indians throughout the Revolution to espouse the British cause.

The establishment of Lewis County in 1816 was followed two years later by that of another county, Preston, formed from Monongalia, lying in the northeast corner of West Virginia, and adjoining Pennsylvania and Maryland. Preston County honored James Patton Preston, Governor of Virginia 1816-1819.

Parts of Greenbrier, Kanawha and Randolph were made into the new county of Nicholas in the same year that Preston was organized. Nicholas lies to the east of Charleston, the capital of West Virginia. Its name derives from Wilson Cary Nicholas, Governor of Virginia 1814-1816, and predecessor of Governor Preston.

1820-1830 Transportation and Communications Improve, Four New Counties

The next county to be created was taken from Hampshire and Berkeley and represented a northern rather than a western expansion. It received the name Morgan from General Daniel

Morgan, one of the outstanding generals of the Revolution who defeated Colonel Tarleton in the Battle of the Cowpens.

The bounds of Morgan County are thus set forth: "Beginning at the mouth of Cherry's Run at the river Potomac in the county of Berkeley, thence up the middle of said Run to its source, thence due west to the top of Sleepy Creek Mountain, thence along the top of said mountain to the line that separates the counties of Frederick and Berkeley, thence with the said line to the county of Hampshire, thence a direct line until it strikes the river Potomac opposite Mitchell's Rock and thence by the river Potomac to the beginning."

Pocahontas County created in 1821, a year after Morgan had been formed, and likewise a West Virginia county, lies in the southeastern section of the state opposite the Virginia county of Alleghany. Its name was a long delayed tribute to the fine character and achievements of the Indian maid Pocahontas. She both aided the settlers at Jamestown with gifts of sorely needed food, and by her marriage to John Rolfe secured eight years of peace for them. This period was vital to their survival.

Pocahontas lies in a mountainous region rich in bituminous coal deposits, so much so that Pocahontas coal is known everywhere. The description of the county's bounds notes the lines of Greenbrier, Bath, Randolph and Pendleton counties and "Randolph court House." This is the first mention of a courthouse anywhere in this area.

After discussing eight counties now in West Virginia, we come to a Virginia county, Alleghany, formed in 1822 from Botetourt, Bath and Monroe counties. It is the name the Delaware Indians gave both the Ohio and the Alleghany rivers, but its origin is uncertain. Presumably, the mountains took their name from the river. Within the bounds of Alleghany County the Jackson and the Cowpasture rivers unite to form the James River, the longest river in the state and the most important in its early history.

Its bounds were thus described: "beginning at the top of the middle of Potts' mountain, where the road leading from Fincastle to the Sweet Springs crosses the same; thence with said road to the top of Peter's mountain; thence a straight line to the Greenbrier county line on the top of the Alleghany mountain so as to pass between the Sweet and Red springs; thence with the top of the Alleghany or Greenbrier line to a certain point so that a straight line drawn thence to include in the new county Captain Henry Massie's plantation in the Falling Spring Valley may also include Archibald Morriss's plantation on Jackson's river in said new county; thence a straight line from the said Massie's across the Cowpasture river immediately below William Griffin's on said river to the Rockbridge county line; thence with said line to a point in the Rockbridge and Botetourt line so that a line drawn from thence will pass at or near the junction of Jackson's and Cowpasture rivers to the nearest part of the Rich Patch mountain; and this line to be so run as to leave the house and yard of Captain John Jordan in the county of Botetourt; thence with the highest points of the said Rich Patch mountain next to Craig's creek so as to include the inhabitants of the Rich Patch in said new county, to a point at which it unites with Potts' mountain, thence with the top of the said mountain to the beginning."

In 1824 the county of Logan was formed from portions of Giles, Cabell, Tazewell and Kanawha counties. It lay in the southwestern part of the present West Virginia not far from the Kentucky line. The name derives from the Mingo Indian chieftain whose famous speech preserved by Thomas Jefferson was long a popular selection for young would-be orators.

1830-1840 Large Increase in Population Necessitates Fourteen New Counties

For seven years, there was no further expansion until in 1831 when the Virginia county of Floyd was formed. This was taken from that part of Montgomery County adjacent to the counties of Franklin, Patrick and Grayson. The name is in honor of John Floyd, Governor of Virginia 1830-1834. It is a beautiful county of high mountains, fertile valleys and good blue-grass pasture land.

Its bounds were thus prescribed: "Beginning at the widow Litterell's, thence a straight line to John Thrasher's; thence a straight line to John Cooper's old place; thence a straight line to where the Waggon road crosses the Laurel ridge; from thence along the highest part of said ridge to Little river; and down the same to Mack's mountain; and with the same to the Grayson line and with the same to the Patrick line and with the same to the Franklin line and with the same to the line of Montgomery and Franklin, opposite the widow Litterell's; from thence a straight line to the beginning."

In addition to Floyd, Fayette County was also formed in 1831. This county, the second attempt Virginia had made to honor the Marquis de la Fayette, fell later into West Virginia. Taken from parts of Logan, Greenbrier, Nicholas and Kanawha, Fayette lies in the southeastern part of the state, and is traversed by the New River.

The lengthy description of its bounds notes several streams besides the New River; namely: Lick creek, Meadow river, Mill creek, Gauley river, Twenty Mile creek, Kanawha river, Guyandotte and Cole (Coal) river. For the first time we find mention of a turnpike, "the Kanawha turnpike." In the decade 1820-1830, a great interest in highways developed, and turnpikes and toll roads became numerous. In Virginia a well-known toll road ran through the Valley of Virginia called "the Valley Pike." National highway Route Number 11 largely follows its path.

The third county created in 1831 also is now a West Virginia county, Jackson. Formed from Mason, Kanawha and Wood, Jackson lies in the western part of the state along the Ohio River south of Parkersburg. It was named for General Andrew Jackson, then in his first term as President of the United States. A song popular at that time carried these two lines complimenting his exploits:

"Glory be to Jackson for the Battle of New Orleans
For there he gave the enemy the hot butter-beans"

referring to his victory over the British in the battle of that name.

We come back to Virginia now and discuss the fourth county created in 1831. Formed from Shenandoah and Rockingham counties, it lies in the Valley of Virginia with the famed Luray Cavern within its borders. It was named in honor of John Page, Governor of Virginia 1802-1805.

Its bounds are as follows: "Beginning at a point in the line of the counties of Rockingham and Orange on the top of the Blue Ridge opposite to the headwaters of Naked creek in the county of Rockingham; thence a straight line to the headwaters of said creek; thence with the meanderings of said creek to its junction with the South river; thence down the bed of said river to the upper end of Michael Shuler's island; thence a straight line to the mouth of Shuler's run; thence with the main branch of said run to its source; thence a straight line to the top of the Massanutten mountain; thence with the top of said mountain to its termination near Daniel Clem's; thence to the top of the eastern Fort mountain; thence with the top of said mountain to a point opposite to the mouth of Cunningham's run in the county of Shenandoah; thence a straight line to the mouth of said run; thence with the said run to its source; thence to a point in a direct line to the top of the Blue Ridge in the line of the two counties of Shenandoah and Culpeper; and thence with the top of the Blue Ridge to the beginning."

From Washington and Wythe in 1832 was established the new county of Smyth situated in the southwestern section of Virginia and extending to the North Carolina line. The name derives from General Alexander Smyth of Wythe County, Inspector General of the Army in 1812 and Member of Congress

1817-1825, 1827-1830. A portrait of him by Saint Memin is in the Corcoran Art Gallery.

The bounds of the county are set forth as follows: "Beginning on the main stage road at a bridge in a hollow at a point where the spring branch of Phillip Griever deceased crosses the same; thence a direct line, passing equidistant between Preston's and King's salt wells to the line of Russell county; and from the said point on the main stage road aforesaid where the said spring branch crosses the same running south twenty-five degrees east to the southern boundary of Washington county; and beginning on the main stage coach road leading by Abingdon and Wythe courthouse, ten miles by the said road dividing Washington and Wythe counties; running thence northwest to the northern boundary of Wythe county and southeast to the southern boundary of Wythe county. The said line through Wythe county running precisely parallel with the line aforesaid through Washington County."

In the above we note the great development that had taken place in this section, a "stagecoach road" and two towns, Abingdon and Wythe Courthouse, being mentioned for the first time. A road over which a heavy stagecoach could travel was a big advance over the bridle paths and "rolling roads" of the preceding century.

In 1833, Rappahannock also a Virginia county, was established. This was taken from Culpeper County and named for the river which traverses it, and which, likely took its name from the Indian tribe living along its banks. The settlers first called this river Pembroke in honor of William Herbert, third Earl of Pembroke and brother-in-law of the famous Sir Philip Sydney. The Earl was a member of the Virginia Company of London and invested four hundred pounds sterling in the enterprise.

The bounds of Rappahannock County were as follows: "Beginning at the corner of Madison and Culpeper counties upon the top of the Blue Ridge of mountains and running thence with the line of said counties to the point where it is intersected by Hugh's river above the junction of Hugh's and Hazel's rivers; thence with Hugh's river to the junction of the aforesaid rivers; thence to a bend in the river near a point called the Giant's castle; thence to Horner's mill upon the Fauquier and Culpeper line; thence with said line to the corner of the aforesaid counties upon the top of the Blue Ridge, thence with said mountain to the beginning."

The next county established in this continuous effort to make due processes of law and order accessible to all lies now in the northern tip of West Virginia. It is called Marshall, honoring John Marshall who died in 1835, the year of the county's creation. John Marshall's career and achievements are too well known to be recounted here; suffice it to say that in his lengthy tenure as its Chief Justice he gave plan, directive and purpose to the Supreme Court of the United States.

The bounds of Marshall County were set forth as being "all that part of the lower end of the county of Ohio lying south of a line beginning on the Ohio river at a stone to be fixed on the bank of said river, one half mile above the mouth of Buggs' run; thence a direct line to the northern boundary of the town of West Union and thence continuing the same course to the Pennsylvania line."

In 1836 Braxton, also at present a West Virginia county, was created from portions of Lewis and Nicholas counties. Its name honors Carter Braxton, a Signer of the Declaration of Independence, the last one of the Virginia signers to receive this distinction.

The description of its bounds though long is of interest because of the number of place names used and is therefore quoted: "beginning at Salt Works road at the head of Barbecue run and running thence with the dividing ridge of the Kanawha and Monongalia waters to the head of the Fall run; thence along the leading ridge to the forks of the Little Kanawha; thence up the right hand fork to its head; thence with the dividing ridge between Kanawha, Buchanan and Elk waters, to the corner of Randolph and Nicholas county line; thence with the said line to the top of the Point mountain above the Fork lick; thence along the top of the Point mountain to the end thereof; thence a straight line to Joseph Priam's (so as to include Joseph Priam's lands within the boundary of the new county); thence a straight line to the top of the ridge between Big and Little Birch rivers, and down said ridge to the mouth of Little Birch river; thence a straight line to the mouth of the Rock-camp fork of Big Buffalo (above Young's Bottoms); thence down the same to its mouth, crossing Elk river; thence to the Lewis and Kanawha county line at a point where a straight line to the mouth of the Long Shoal run will include Jacob Shock on Steer creek within the boundary of the new county; thence up the said Long Shoal run to the top of the ridge between the Sand fork and Little Kanawha; thence with the dividing ridge to the head of the left hand fork of the Three lick fork of Oil creek; thence to its mouth; thence to the main fork of Oil creek; thence up the Clover lick fork to the beginning."

From almost the center of the present state of West Virginia, we now return to Virginia and note the creation from Frederick of the new county of Clarke. Braxton, Clarke and Warren were all established in the year 1836. Clarke, though incorrectly spelled pays honor to that native of Albemarle County who won the Northwest Territory for the Continental Congress, George Rogers Clark. The county, cut from the eastern part of Frederick, adjoins Jefferson, Loudoun and Fauquier.

Its bounds are thus given: "Beginning at the point in the Blue Ridge where the line dividing the counties of Jefferson and Loudoun meets the line dividing the counties of Frederick and Loudoun, thence with the line dividing the counties of Jefferson and Frederick to the middle of the Opequon creek; thence up the middle of the Opequon to the mouth of Wright's branch; thence up that stream to the mouth of Nations Spring run;

thence a direct line until it reaches Colin Leach's corner, next to major Seth Mason's land on the road to Nineveh; thence eastwardly by a direct line, passing south of the buildings and curtilages of doctor James Hay and James M. Hite, to a point on the Shenandoah river, at the mouth of Fauntleroy's mill run, on the north side of the Shenandoah river; thence from the mouth of said run a straight line to the nearest top of the Blue Ridge of mountains; and thence on the eastern boundary of Frederick county to the beginning."

Curtilage, used for the first time in any description, is a law term denoting the fenced-in area adjoining a dwelling house or a courtyard. The term often used now is dependencies.

Warren, the third county created in 1836, lies over the Blue Ridge from and a little to the south of Clarke. Its territory was taken from those portions of Shenandoah and Frederick counties that adjoined "the counties of Rappahannock and Fauquier in the southern part thereof." The name honors the brave soldier Major General Joseph Warren who fell in the Battle of Bunker Hill.

The bounds of Warren County which mention some places noted in Clarke County's bounds are as follows: "Beginning at the top of the Blue Ridge where the counties of Shenandoah and Page corner on the Rappahannock county line; thence west with the Page line to the top of the southeast Fort mountain; thence north with the top of said mountain to its termination at the mouth of Powel's fort; thence a straight line from the top of said mountain to the nearest top of the Three top mountain; thence with the top of said mountain to the high peak opposite Strasburg; thence a straight line to Hoffman's ford across the north branch of Shenandoah river; thence down the bed of said river to the mouth of Cedar creek on the north side of said river; thence up said creek to where the Winchester and Staunton stage road crosses said creek; thence a straight line to Zion meeting-house in Frederick county; thence with the main road leading towards the White post until it reaches Colin Leache's corner, a point on said road; then eastwardly by a direct line passing south of the buildings and curtilages of doctor James Hay and James M. Hite; to a point on Burden's March run; thence by a direct line to a point on the Shenandoah river at the mouth of Fauntleroy's mill run on the north side of the Shenandoah river; thence from the mouth of said run a straight line to the nearest top of the Blue Ridge; thence a southwest course with the top of said Blue Ridge to the beginning."

The next year, 1837, Mercer, now in West Virginia but adjoining Giles County, Virginia, was formed. The Act authorizing its creation is as follows: "All that part of the counties of Giles and Tazewell contained within the following boundary lines . . . shall form one distinct and new county and be called and known by the name of Mercer county in memory of general Hugh Mercer who fell at Princeton." Appropriately the county seat of Mercer County is Princeton.

In 1838 the Virginia counties of Greene and Roanoke were set up.

The Act for the former county is as follows: "So much of the county of Orange as it lies next to and adjoining the counties of Madison, Rockingham and Albemarle and west of a line beginning at Cave's old mill (now James Jackson's) on the Madison county line and running thence a straight line to where Whitelow's mill run intersects the Albemarle county line shall form one distinct and new county and be called and known by the name of Greene county in memory of general Nathaniel Greene who served his country in the revolutionary war."

It may be mentioned that this is the second county in Virginia honoring General Greene. The correct spelling for his first name is Nathanael.

In Greene County lies Swift Run Gap. This is the gap in the Blue Ridge mountains over which in September 1715, Governor Spotswood led his adventurous band into the beautiful Valley of Virginia. Westward expansion began at this date.

The second county created in 1838 was Roanoke composed of that portion of Botetourt lying next to the southwestern parts of Montgomery, Franklin and Bedford. Roanoke was the name applied by the early colonists to the shell-beads of different colors used by the Indians as a medium of exchange. The river had long been known as Roanoke, hence it seems likely that the county took its name from the river.

Roanoke County is thus bounded: "beginning at a point on the Blue ridge which divides the counties of Bedford and Botetourt, thence northwest to the house now the residence of John Bonsack on Glade creek so as to include the said Bonsack in the new county, thence a line to the house of Thomas Barnes including said Barnes in the county, and so as to leave John W. Thompson in the county of Botetourt, thence a straight line crossing the Catawba Valley at a point one mile due north of Mrs. Garwood's; thence crossing Craig's creek (passing the house of John Spessard on Craig's creek so as to leave the said Spessard in the old county) to the top of the mountain which divides the waters of Craig's creek and Sinking creek, thence westwardly along the top of the mountain to the point where the lines of Botetourt, Montgomery and Giles counties meet, thence with the line which divided the county of Botetourt from the county of Montgomery to the point at which the said line joins the Bedford line, thence with the Bedford line to the beginning."

In this same area in the following year the county of Pulaski was created from the western end of Montgomery and the eastern end of Wythe. Its name honored the Polish patriot Count Casimir Pulaski who, exiled from his homeland, came to America and joined General Washington's army. He participated in important engagements and finally fell on 11 October 1779 unsuccessfully defending Savannah, Georgia.

The bounds of Pulaski County are thus set forth: "beginning

at a line dividing the county of Giles from Montgomery on New river, thence with same line to the head of a hollow above Hiram Davis's on Little Walker's creek; thence to a point on the main road between the lands of John T. Sayers and Harvey Shepherd including the plantation of David G. Shepherd, thence to the mouth of Pine run on New river, thence to the Grayson county line; including Sally King's plantation on Reed island; thence with the Grayson line to the Floyd line, and with the same to the mouth of Indian creek on Little river, and with the same including the farm of Creed Taylor to New river, and with the same to the beginning."

1840-1850 FLOOD TIDE, SIXTEEN NEW COUNTIES

Three years elapsed before another county was needed and it was not until 1842 that the county of Marion was formed from the southern part of Monongalia and the northern part of Harrison. The name given it was "in honor to and in memory of general Francis Marion who served his country in the war of the revolution." This county now lies in West Virginia.

Also in 1842, a new county in the southwestern area of Virginia was formed from Grayson. It was thus bounded: "beginning on the North Carolina line at or near Fisher's peak and running thence a straight line across the said county of Grayson (so as to cross Chestnut creek near the ford at major James Anderson's) to the line of Wythe county thence along said Wythe line to the line of Pulaski county thence along said Pulaski line to line of Floyd county, thence along said Floyd line to the line of Patrick; thence along the said Patrick line to the North Carolina line thence along said North Carolina line to the point of beginning . . . and be called and known by the name of Carroll in memory of Charles Carroll of Carrollton." Charles Carroll, one of the Maryland Signers of the Declaration of Independence, had been the last survivor of this noble group, dying in 1832 at the age of 95 years.

65

The third county created in 1842, Wayne, taken from the western part of Cabell lay along the Ohio river and is now in West Virginia. This new division was to "be called and known by the name of Wayne county in memory and in honor of general Anthony Wayne."

Two counties destined to be in West Virginia were set up in 1843. The first of these was Ritchie in the western part of the state created from portions of Lewis, Harrison and Wood. The name honors Thomas Ritchie, "founder and long the able editor of the *Richmond Enquirer* and 'father of democracy' in Virginia."

The other county, Barbour, lying in the northeastern part of the state was established from areas of Harrison, Lewis and Randolph. The description of its bounds besides mentioning the usual rivers and ridges names also several persons which always draws the reader's interest. Some of these are: "Rueben Davisson's farm," "the old farm now occupied by Samuel Bartlett," "William Bean's," "Samuel Black's residence" and "the widow Corley's corner tree."

The name of the county was "in honour to and in memory of Philip Barbour of Virginia." Appropriately the county seat is Philippi. Judge Barbour, a native of Orange County, Virginia, where his home "Frascati" still stands, achieved distinction as a Judge of the Supreme Court. He had died the year before the county was formed.

Taylor County, also in the northeastern part of West Virginia was formed in 1844 from sections of Harrison, Barbour and Marion. Its bounds mention "the residence of Anderson Corbin," "the residence of James M'Daniell," "the residence of Joseph Bailey," "the farm of John H. Woodford" and others.

The name of the county honors General Zachary Taylor, twelfth President of the United States, a native of Orange County, Virginia. He had a distinguished military career, serving in the Black Hawk, Seminole and Mexican Wars.

The determination on the part of Virginia's General Assembly to render justice more easy and accessible to all its citizens was as strong in 1845 when parts of Lewis and Kanawha counties became Gilmer County as it had been two centuries earlier. It was the unifying purpose in all development.

The name Gilmer takes us to Albemarle County, Virginia, where Thomas Walker Gilmer, elected Governor of Virginia in 1840, was born. He was grandson of Doctor Thomas Walker of "Castle Hill," Albemarle County who was the first to explore Southwest Virginia and Kentucky.

At the same time that Gilmer was formed, the county which lies to the north of it was established. Both are now in West Virginia. The bounds of Doddridge County, as noted in the Act of Assembly creating it, list several waterways including Hughes's and Monongahela rivers but the most interesting land mark named is "the Northwestern turnpike road at tollgate number eleven." This shows steadily advancing development in transportation, for earlier there had been references to wagon roads, then to stagecoach roads and now to a turnpike with the regular tollgates to provide funds for maintenance.

The name honors the memory of Philip Doddridge of Brooke County, who was a prominent member of the Virginia Constitutional Convention of 1829-30. He was an advocate of the wishes of the western portion of the state to have representation based upon white population exclusively. This motion failed and a compromise constitution was agreed upon. Philip Doddridge died in Washington, D. C. in 1832 while serving as a member of Congress.

After discussing six counties now in West Virginia, we come now to the county of Appomattox formed in 1845 from portions of Buckingham, Prince Edward, Charlotte and Campbell. The name derives from the river which traverses the county.

Its bounds are thus defined: "Beginning at the mouth of David's creek on James river; thence a straight line to the head of Holleway creek; thence down the same as it meanders to Appomattox river; thence down the same to the Cutbanks; thence a straight line to the mouth of Cabin branch on Vaughan's creek; thence up the said creek to its head; thence a straight line to Merryman's or Land's; thence along the public road leading by M'Kinney's old store to the fork of the Lynchburg road about a mile north of the Red house; thence a straight line to the old mill formerly owned by William Harvey; thence along the Lynchburg road to the mill formerly owned by Samuel Branch, esquire, on Falling river; thence up the said river to the mouth of Reedy creek; thence a straight line to Hunter's old tavern (now Glovers); thence a straight line to Sterling C. Anderson's; thence a straight line to the mouth of Scott's branch about a mile before the mouth of Joshua's creek on James river; and thence down the said river to the beginning."

In 1846, in the northwestern portion of the present state of West Virginia, the new county of Wetzel was set up from Tyler. The following landowners are named as living within its bounds: "James Peden (or Paden), Richard Anchrom and Rueben Martin, esquire." The county was so called "in honor of Louis Wetzel, the distinguished frontiersman and Indian scout, the Boone of Northwestern Virginia."

As if feeling this action a little unfair, the Assembly next year, when a new county was to be created, named it Boone "in honor to and in memory of Daniel Boone the well known pioneer of the western frontier settlements." Boone was taken from parts of Kanawha, Cabell and Logan counties and lies south of Charleston, the state capital.

In this same year, the county of Alexandria was added to Virginia's jurisdiction. The Assembly enacted "That the territory comprising the county of Alexandria in the District of Columbia heretofore ceded by this commonwealth to the United States and by an act of congress approved on the ninth day of July eighteen hundred and forty-six retroceded to this commonwealth, and by it accepted, is hereby declared to be an integral portion of this

68

commonwealth and the citizens thereof are hereby declared to be subject to all the provisions, and entitled to all the benefits, rights and privileges of the bill of rights and constitution of this commonwealth."

In 1791, to aid in establishing the Federal City, as Washington was sometimes called, Virginia gave to the United States certain land taken from Fairfax County to form a part of the District of Columbia. In the Act quoted above it has been seen that the United States retroceded to Virginia that part of the District of Columbia which comprised the county of Alexandria. The name in 1920 was changed to Arlington.

Across the state from Alexandria the new county of Highland came into being in 1847, being taken from parts of Pendleton and Bath. Its bounds are thus given: "Beginning where the North river gap road crosses the Augusta county line, and running thence to the top of Jackson's mountain so as to leave Jacob Hiver's mansion house in Pendleton county; thence to Andrew Fleisher's so as to include his mansion house in the new county; thence to the highlands between the Dry run and Crab bottom; and thence along the top of the High Knob; thence north sixty-five degrees west to Pocahontas county line; thence along said county line to the plum orchard on the top of the Alleghany mountains; thence to Adam Stephenson's mansion house on Jackson's river in Bath county so as to include Thomas Campbell's mansion house on Back creek and also said Adam Stephenson's in the new county; thence to Andrew H. Byrd's mansion house on the Cowpasture river so as to include the same in the new county, and so as to leave the dwelling house of William M'Clintick, jr. in Bath county; thence south sixty-five degrees east to the Augusta county line and thence with said line to the beginning."

The name of the county is derived from its exceptionally high altitude, and the name of its county seat, Monterey, reflects the popular interest felt in the victory General Taylor had just won over the Mexicans at the Battle of Monterey.

After the formation of Highland County five counties destined to lie in West Virginia were established. The first of these, Hancock, created in 1848 out of Brooke, lies in the extreme northern tip of the present state between the Ohio river and the Pennsylvania state line. Its name honors the first Signer of the Declaration of Independence, whose distinguished signature is familiar through countless reproductions.

In this same year from portions of Jackson and Wood counties was formed Wirt. This is in the northwestern area of the state not far from Parkersburg. In the description of bounds, only three land owners are named, John Stephens, junior, John P. Thomasson and William Goff.

The name of the county honored the distinguished lawyer, William Wirt, who had died a few years before. He had served as Attorney General of the United States from 1817 to 1829 and had been a candidate for the Presidency on the Anti-Masonic ticket in 1832. He is best remembered for his life of Patrick Henry.

The third county created in 1848 was Putnam, composed of parts of Kanawha, Cabell and Mason counties, and lying to the west of the city of Charleston. Its name recalls a hero of the Revolutionary War, General Israel Putnam who distinguished himself at the Battle of Bunker Hill and became a popular hero.

1850-1860 EBBING TIDE, TWELVE COUNTIES

The year 1850 saw the formation of two more counties now in West Virginia. The first one, Raleigh, was taken from the southern part of Fayette. In its bounds, the lands of Isaac Sonners and Jackson Jarrell, and the New, Coal, and Guyandotte rivers are noted. The name was "in memory of Sir Walter Raleigh who made the earliest effort to colonize Virginia." It is pleasant to see that Virginia finally recognized her debt to this valiant soul, even though it was tardily done, for he died in 1618.

A few days after Raleigh became a county, the Virginia Assembly enacted that the county of Wyoming be erected out of the county of Logan. Wyoming lies in the southern central portion of West Virginia. The reason for the name is obscure, whether it was for the beautiful Wyoming Valley in north central Pennsylvania watered by the Susquehanna River, or for the brutal massacre of its inhabitants on 4 July 1778 by a British and Indian force is unknown.

Half of the nineteenth century has passed and our narrative has only a few more years to chronicle. In 1851, three counties were formed. One of these, Craig, remained in Virginia. It was taken from parts of Botetourt, Roanoke, Giles and Monroe.

Its bounds were as follows: "Beginning on the top of the Middle mountain at the corner of Monroe and Alleghany counties, near Achilles Dews, and running with the Alleghany line to the top of Peters' mountain; thence westward along the top of said mountain to a point nearby opposite to the house of Boston Rowan; thence crossing Potts' creek to a point one fourth of a mile below said Rowan's so as to leave said Rowan's in the county of Monroe; thence a southwestern direction to the top of Potts' mountain, so as to leave Armentrout, Fridley and Rose in Monroe; thence westward along the top of said mountain to a point opposite Colonel R. M. Hutchinson's on John's creek, and thence a straight line including said Hutchinson in the new county, and crossing Sinking creek valley to William Niday's, including said Niday in the new county, to the Montgomery line; thence eastward with the Montgomery line to the corner of Roanoke and Montgomery; thence with the Roanoke line to the top of Brush mountain; thence eastward along said mountain, crossing the Cove branch where John Carper formerly lived; thence along the same range of mountains passing near Lilburn Doss's, crossing Stone Coal gap; thence along the same range of mountains, crossing Price's turnpike road to a point opposite Daniel Sizer's; thence a northwestern direction crossing Craig's creek above said Sizer's to a point one mile from Craig's creek on the ridge; thence to Andrew Persinger's on Barber's creek; thence to the Alleghany line and with the same to the beginning."

The name of the county honored Robert Craig, member of Congress from Virginia 1829-1834, 1835-1841.

In the same month in which Craig was set up, the new county of Upshur was created from parts of Randolph, Barbour and Lewis, all now in West Virginia. The starting point in the description of its bounds reads as follows: "Beginning at a rock or milestone on the Staunton and Parkersburg turnpike road ten miles east of Weston in Lewis County." This shows that transportation had developed sufficiently to connect places on the Ohio River with other sections of Virginia.

Upshur County took its name from Abel P. Upshur whom President Tyler appointed Secretary of State to succeed Daniel Webster. Upshur was killed 28 February 1844 by the explosion of a new type of cannon which was being tested on the U.S.S. *Princeton.*

Also in March 1851, from the counties of Tyler, Wood and Ritchie the new county of Pleasants was established. This lies in the area around Parkersburg in the northwestern part of West Virginia, along the Ohio River. The name honored the memory of James Pleasants, Governor of Virginia, 1822 to 1825, member of a family long resident and prominent in the state.

Five years passed and in the interval population had increased to such an extent in the western part of Virginia that four county governments had to be set up to take care of legal needs. One of these, Wise, formed from portions of Lee, Scott and Russell counties, remains in Virginia. The name honored Henry A. Wise, Governor of Virginia 1856-1860.

The bounds of the county were as follows: "Beginning at the break of Cumberland mountain on the Kentucky and Virginia line where the Pound fork of Sandy breaks through the Cumberland mountain; thence up the Pound fork to the mouth of Crane's nest, a water of said Pound fork; thence with the dividing ridge between the waters of Crane's nest and McLure's, to William Taylor's farm, including said Taylor's farm in the new county; thence a straight line to the mouth of Lick creek; thence down Clinch river to the mouth of Guest's river; thence up Guest's river one mile; thence a straight line to the Camp rock south of the High Knob; thence a straight line to the Pole fence on Little Powell's mountain, on the line dividing Scott and Lee counties; thence with said county line to the head of Stock creek including the farm of Zachariah N. Wells in the said county; thence a straight line to the Cedar gap near Powell's river; thence a straight line to the dividing ridge between the waters of Crab orchard and Pigeon fork; thence with said dividing ridge to the Kentucky line and thence with the Kentucky line to the beginning."

In the Act creating the county it was ordered that the "said seat of justice shall be known as Gladesville," but the present county seat is called Wise.

As has been said, Wise was the only one of the four counties erected in 1856 that remains in Virginia. The next county formed was Calhoun taken from the lower portion of Gilmer County beginning at the West Fork of the Little Kanawha River. The name derives from the great South Carolina statesman who succeeded Abel P. Upshur as Secretary of State and was long outstanding in politics.

At the same time that Calhoun became an entity, parts of the counties of Kanawha, Jackson, and Gilmer lying a little to the west of Calhoun became Roane County. The description of its bounds is startling when it mentions "the Ravenswood and California turnpike in Jackson county," but later we learn that California is a town in Jackson County.

With regard to Roane County, "its name and that of its seat of justice, Spencer, commemorate that of him [Spencer Roane] whose life and public services added lustre to the annals of Virginia jurisprudence." Spencer Roane was "judge of the Supreme Bench 1794 to 1822."

The next county was Tucker formed out of the northeastern portion of Randolph County and adjoining also the counties of Hardy, Preston and Pendleton. The county seat appropriately bore the name of Saint George. The county was "named in honor of Saint George Tucker the eminent Virginia jurist while the seat of justice derives its name from Saint George Tucker who was Clerk of the House of Delegates at the time the county was formed."

Two years later in 1858, three more counties were established, one of which, Buchanan, was destined to remain in Virginia, and the other two in West Virginia.

Mc Dowell, one of the two, was taken from the northwest portion of Tazewell County and remains a border county between the two states, "The ridge between Abb's Valley and Sandy" is one of the bounding lines noted in the description; it recalls the Indian Massacre that occurred in that Valley and the many stories related about it.

The name of the county honors James Mc Dowell, elected Governor of Virginia in 1843 and serving until 1846.

Clay County formed also in 1858 was created out of the southern part of Braxton County and the northern part of Nicholas. Among the property owners whose lands were mentioned as within its bounds, were Thomas Jarvis, jr., James Rogers, Charles Ruffner, who with others owned a twelve thousand acre tract "(near the farm of William Nichol, Sr.)," Strother B. Grose and Abraham Dilly.

The county was so named in honor of Henry Clay, the great Kentucky statesman who had died only a few years before its formation.

The Virginia county established in 1858 from parts of Taze-

74

well and Russell was Buchanan, named for James Buchanan, President of the United States 1857-1861.

Its bounds were as follows: "Beginning at the state line between Kentucky and Virginia and with said line to its intersection with the line of Wise county, to the top of the dividing ridge between the waters of Sandy and Clinch and with said ridge eastwardly to the head of Dismal, a branch of the Lavica fork of Sandy river; then with the dividing ridge between the waters of Dismal and the waters of the Dry fork of Sandy and with the ridge between the waters of the Lavica fork and the Dry fork to the ridge between Knox creek and Bull creek to Tug river and down Tug river to the beginning."

1860-1870 Recession, Two Counties

In 1860, an Act was passed to create the new county of Webster from portions of the counties of Nicholas, Braxton and Randolph, all to be later in West Virginia. The name honored Daniel Webster, the prominent statesman who had died only a few years previously.

In March 1861, the new county of Bland, taken from portions of Giles, Wythe and Tazewell and named for Richard Bland of Revolutionary War fame came into being. Its bounds are thus set forth: "beginning at the top of Walker's Little mountain at the line between Wythe and Pulaski and running northwards with said line of Pulaski, to the top of Walker's Big mountain; thence eastward along the top of said last mentioned mountain to a point opposite the mouth of Kimberling creek; thence by a line northward passing through the mouth of said Kimberling creek to a point on the top of the mountain which lies south of Wolf creek, three miles east of the present county line between Giles and Tazewell counties; thence to a point on the top of East river mountain two miles east of the present county line between Giles and Tazewell so as to include the homestead of

Madison Allen and his lands adjoining thereto; thence with the top of the said East River mountain westward to a point two miles west of George Steel's house on Clear fork; thence across and by a line as near as may be at right angles to the course of the valley between to the top of Rich mountain and westward along the top of said Rich mountain so far as to include the settlement of Wolf creek, thence across the top of Garden mountain; thence along the top of Garden mountain to a point through which the line between Wythe and Smyth would pass if prolonged; thence by said prolonged line to the said line between Wythe and Smyth and by the last mentioned line to the top of Walker's Big mountain; thence eastward with the top of said Walker's Big mountain to a point opposite the headwaters of Walker's Little creek; thence across to the top of Walker's Little mountain, thence to the top of said mountain eastward to the beginning."

Hardly was the ink dry on the Act quoted above when war precluded further settlements and expansion. Not for nearly twenty years would another and the last county be established.

FINIS — ONE COUNTY

In March 1880, out of the counties of Russell, Wise, and Buchanan was formed the new county of Dickenson, named for a prominent member of the Readjuster Party, then dominant in Virginia.

Its bounds noted in great detail are as follows: "beginning at Osborn's gap in Cumberland mountain on the state line; thence a straight line to the top of George's Fork mountain at a point where the road crosses said mountain; thence with the top of the mountain to the head of Lick branch, a tributary of Crane's nest creek; thence a straight line to the mouth of Birchfield creek; thence up Crane's Nest creek to the mouth of Lion's fork; thence up said creek to the forks of said branch; thence up the Fork spur to the top of Crane's Nest bridge; thence a straight line to Sandy Ridge meeting-house in the county of Wise on the top of Sandy Ridge; thence with the top of Sandy ridge to the James Porter farm at the head of Nancy's ridge; thence a straight line to Trammel gap on Sandy ridge, thence with the top of Sandy ridge with a line of Russell county to the James P. Kiser farm, thence a straight line to Henry Kiser's farm on the top of Sandy ridge at the Russell county line; thence with the Russell county line to James Rasnaker's farm, including said farm in the new county; thence down the Cany ridge to the mouth of Cany creek; thence down Indian creek to its mouth; including J. H. Duly's farm; thence down Russell's fork of Sandy river to the mouth of Panpan creek, including Andrew Owen's dwelling house; thence a straight line to the mouth of Greenbrier creek, a tributary of Prater creek; thence a straight line to the Big meadow gap; thence down a branch to Gressy creek; thence down said creek to the mouth of Russell's fork of Sandy river; thence down said river to the state line of Virginia and Kentucky; thence with the state line to the beginning."

The formation of Dickenson County in 1880 completed all the local organizations authorized by the Virginia Assembly from 1634 up to the present, though in many counties minor changes in bounds have been enacted from time to time.

We have seen the little feeble settlements along the James River extend like a rising tide now east, now south, now north and finally with great impetus to the west. Each settlement as it was established proceeded to put into effect the concepts of law and order as practiced at Jamestown, and handed down from father to son. The principle of representative constitutional government as evidenced in the first General Assembly of 1619 may be called the sacred fire each settlement took with it and carefully tended. It was the one thing all shared whether they lived by the James River or high on the Blue Ridge. A settlement, a county, a state, each one must have law, order, ready justice, representative government. That is the theme underlying the development of Virginia which we have traced step by step. It is the theme underlying the development of our nation. Every American is a debtor to Jamestown for his heritage of representative constitutional government.

BIBLIOGRAPHY

Acts of the General Assembly of Virginia, 1808-1880.

Daniel, J. R. V., *A Hornbook of Virginia History,* Richmond, 1950.

Hening, William Waller, *The Statutes at Large,* Being *a Collection of All the Laws of Virginia,* 1619-1792, Richmond, 1809-1823, 13 Vols.

Robinson, Morgan P., *Virginia Counties, Bulletin of the Virginia State Library,* Vol. 9, Nos. 1, 2, 3, 1916.

Shepherd, Samuel, *Statutes at Large,* 1793-1806. Continuation of Hening. Richmond 1835-1836. 3 Vols.

Stith, William. *History of First Discovery and Settlement of Virginia.* Williamsburg, 1747.

Tyler, Lyon G., *Cradle of the Republic.* 2 ed. Richmond, 1900.

KEY TO CHARTS

81

CHART 1

Accawmack —— Northampton —— Accomack
1634-1642/3(Ex.)   1642/3   1662

CHART 2

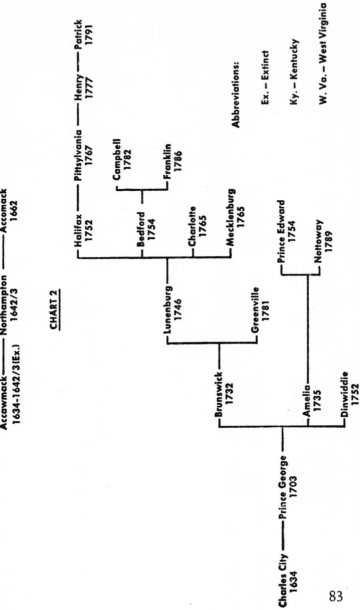

Charles City —— Prince George
1634   1703

Brunswick
1732

Lunenburg
1746

Greenville
1781

Halifax
1752

Bedford
1754

Charlotte
1765

Mecklenburg
1765

Pittsylvania
1767

Campbell
1782

Franklin
1786

Henry
1777

Patrick
1791

Amelia
1735

Dinwiddie
1752

Prince Edward
1754

Nottoway
1789

Abbreviations:

Ex. – Extinct

Ky. – Kentucky

W. Va. – West Virginia

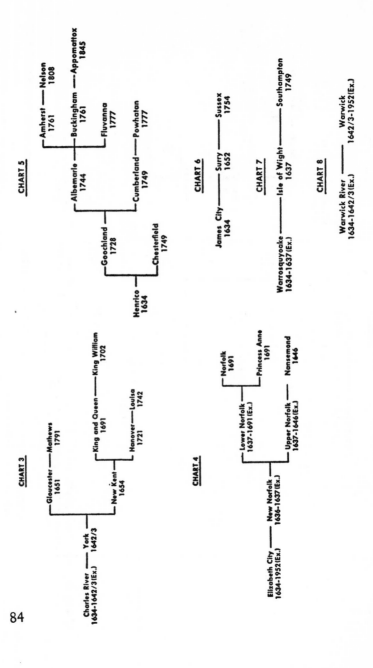

CHART 3

Charles River — York
1634-1642/3(Ex.) 1642/3

Gloucester — Mathews
1651 1791

King and Queen — King William
1691 1702

New Kent
1654

Hanover — Louisa
1721 1742

CHART 4

Elizabeth City — New Norfolk
1634-1952(Ex.) 1636-1637(Ex.)

Lower Norfolk
1637-1691(Ex.)

Norfolk
1691

Princess Anne
1691

Upper Norfolk
1637-1646(Ex.)

Nansemond
1646

CHART 5

Henrico
1634

Goochland
1728

Chesterfield
1749

Albemarle
1744

Cumberland
1749

Amherst — Nelson
1761 1808

Buckingham — Appomattox
1761 1845

Fluvanna
1777

Powhatan
1777

CHART 6

James City — Surry — Sussex
1634 1652 1754

CHART 7

Warrosquyoake — Isle of Wight — Southampton
1634-1637(Ex.) 1637 1749

CHART 8

Warwick River — Warwick
1634-1642/3(Ex.) 1642/3-1952(Ex.)

84

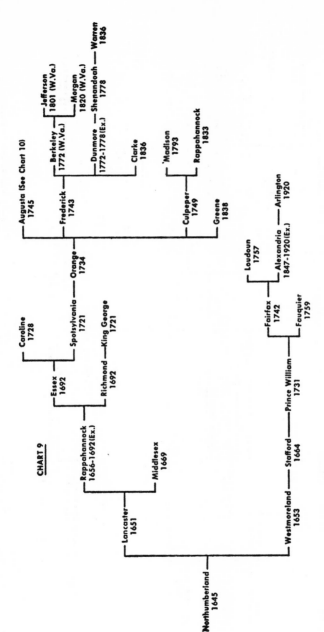

CHART 9

Northumberland 1645

Lancaster 1651

Rappahannock 1656-1692(Ex.)

Middlesex 1669

Essex 1692

Richmond — King George 1692 · 1721

Caroline 1728

Spotsylvania 1721

Orange 1734

Augusta (See Chart 10) 1745

Frederick 1743

Berkeley 1772 (W.Va.)

Jefferson 1801 (W.Va.)

Morgan 1820 (W.Va.)

Dunmore 1772-1778(Ex.)

Shenandoah 1778

Warren 1836

Clarke 1836

Culpeper 1749

'Madison 1793

Rappahannock 1833

Greene 1838

Westmoreland 1653

Stafford 1664

Prince William 1731

Fairfax 1742

Fauquier 1759

Loudoun 1757

Alexandria 1847-1920(Ex.)

Arlington 1920

85

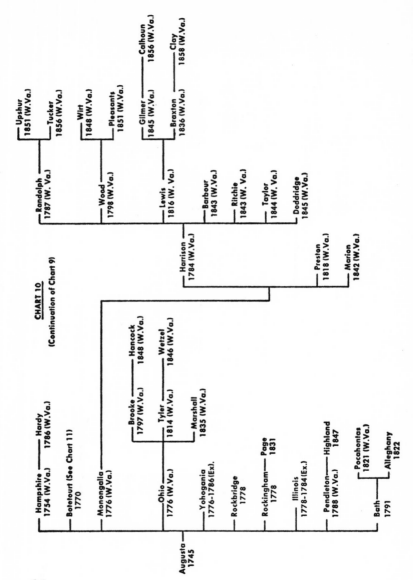

CHART 10
(Continuation of Chart 9)

Upshur
1851 (W.Va.)

Tucker
1856 (W.Va.)

Wirt
1848 (W.Va.)

Pleasants
1851 (W.Va.)

Gilmer
1845 (W.Va.)

Calhoun
1856 (W.Va.)

Braxton
1836 (W.Va.)

Clay
1858 (W.Va.)

Randolph
1787 (W.Va.)

Wood
1798 (W.Va.)

Lewis
1816 (W.Va.)

Barbour
1843 (W.Va.)

Ritchie
1843 (W.Va.)

Taylor
1844 (W.Va.)

Doddridge
1845 (W.Va.)

Harrison
1784 (W.Va.)

Preston
1818 (W.Va.)

Marion
1842 (W.Va.)

Hancock
1848 (W.Va.)

Wetzel
1846 (W.Va.)

Brooke
1797 (W.Va.)

Tyler
1814 (W.Va.)

Marshall
1835 (W.Va.)

Hampshire
1754 (W.Va.)

Hardy
1786 (W.Va.)

Botetourt (See Chart 11)
1770

Monongalia
1776 (W.Va.)

Ohio
1776 (W.Va.)

Yohogania
1776-1786(Ex).

Rockbridge
1778

Rockingham
1778

Page
1831

Illinois
1778-1784(Ex.)

Pendleton
1788 (W.Va.)

Highland
1847

Pocahontas
1821 (W.Va.)

Bath
1791

Alleghany
1822

Augusta
1745

86

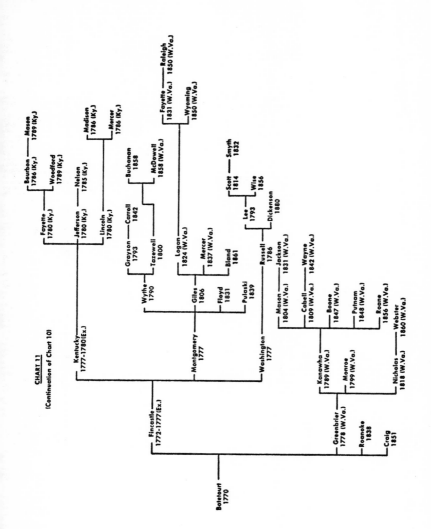

CHART 11
(Continuation of Chart 10)

Boteourt
1770

Fincastle
1772-1777(Ex.)

Kentucky
1777-1780(Ex.)

Fayette
1780 (Ky.)

Bourbon
1786 (Ky.)

Mason
1789 (Ky.)

Woodford
1789 (Ky.)

Jefferson
1780 (Ky.)

Nelson
1785 (Ky.)

Madison
1786 (Ky.)

Lincoln
1780 (Ky.)

Mercer
1786 (Ky.)

Montgomery
1777

Wythe
1790

Grayson
1793

Carroll
1842

Buchanan
1858

McDowell
1858 (W.Va.)

Giles
1806

Tazewell
1800

Floyd
1831

Logan
1824 (W.Va.)

Mercer
1837 (W.Va.)

Pulaski
1839

Bland
1861

Washington
1777

Russell
1786

Lee
1793

Scott
1814

Smyth
1832

Dickenson
1880

Wise
1856

Fayette
1831 (W.Va.)

Raleigh
1850 (W.Va.)

Wyoming
1850 (W.Va.)

Greenbrier
1778 (W.Va.)

Roanoke
1838

Craig
1851

Kanawha
1789 (W.Va.)

Mason
1804 (W.Va.)

Jackson
1831 (W.Va.)

Cabell
1809 (W.Va.)

Wayne
1842 (W.Va.)

Monroe
1799 (W.Va.)

Boone
1847 (W.Va.)

Putnam
1848 (W.Va.)

Nicholas
1818 (W.Va.)

Roane
1856 (W.Va.)

Webster
1860 (W.Va.)

87

INDEX

Charlotte county, 33, 42, 67
Charlottesville, 33
Charters of Virginia, 2, 5, 44
Cheat river, 47
Cherry's run, 55
Chesapeake bay, 18, 51
Chesterfield, Philip D. Stanhope, 4th Earl of, 28
Chesterfield county, 27, 28, 39
Chester's gap, 35
Chestnut creek, 65
Chickacoan, 12
Choppawomsick creek, 21
Christ Church parish, Lancaster county, 15, 16
Christ Church parish, Middlesex county, 16
Chuckatuck creek, 6
Chumley's branch, 20
Cities (political division), 2
Claiborne, William, 3, 13, 14
Clark, George Rogers, 41, 44, 61
Clarke county, 61, 62
Clay, Henry, 74
Clay county, 74
Clear fork, 52, 75
Clem, Daniel, 58
Clinch, 75
Clinch mountain, 45, 48, 50, 53
Clinch river, 38, 50, 53, 73, 75
Clinton, Henry, Sir, 42
Clover Lick fork, 61
Coal (Cole) river, 57, 70
Cole, Richard, 12
Cole (Coal) river, 57, 70
College, at Henrico, 28
Common Pleas courts see Courts, common pleas
Compasses, mariners', 3
Convention, 1775 and 1776, 36, 37
Conway river, 27
Cooper, John, 57
Coppohawk river, 30
Corbin, Anderson, 66
Corley (Mrs.), 66
Cornstalk (Indian), 54
Cornwall parish, 33

Cornwallis, Charles, 2nd Earl, 1st Marquis, 42, 43
Corporations, 1, 2
Cotton, in Southampton county, 28
Council, 2, 9, 20
  Minutes, 9
Counties (political division), 2
  division of Colony into, 3
County courts see Courts, county
"Court Party", 5
Courts, admiralty, in England, 8; in Virginia, 10
  chancery, in England, 8
  common pleas, in England 8
  county, in Virginia, 2, 7, 8, 10
  ecclesiastical, in England, 8
  general court, in Virginia, 8, 9
  inferior, in Virginia, 2, 7
  king's bench, in England, 8
  magistrate's or justice, in Virginia, 7, 8
  monthly, in England, 8, 9; in Virginia, 7, 8, 9, 10
  of exchequer, in England, 8
  parish, in Virginia, 7
  prerogative, in England, 9
Cove branch, 71
Cove creek, 50
Cowpasture river, 40, 47, 55, 56, 69
Cowpens, Battle of, 55
Crab bottom, 69
Crab orchard, 73
Craig, Robert, 72
Craig county, 71, 72
Craig's creek, 56, 64, 71
Crane creek, 52
Crane's nest bridge, 76
Crane's nest creek, 73, 76
Crane's nest river, 72, 73
Crany point, 11
Crayford, England, 13
Cripple creek, 48
Crooked run, 49
Crosses in Fairy Stone Park, 47
Culberson's creek, 36
Culloden, Battle of, 21
Culpeper, Thomas, Lord, 27

92

Russell parish, 30
Russell's fork, 77

Sail's creek, 29
St. Andrew's parish (Brunswick county), 24
St. Anne's parish, 33
Saint George, 74
St. James parish, 33
St. John's parish (New Kent county), 16
St. Mark's parish, 23
St. Memin, Julien F. de, 59
St. Paul's parish (New Kent county), 19
St. Peter's parish (New Kent county), 16
Salt works road, 60
Sand fork, 61
Sandy creek, 38
Sandy Point, 6
Sandy ridge, 76, 77
Sandy river, 72, 74, 75, 77
Sandys, Edwin, Sir, 5
Savannah, Ga., 64
Sayers, John T., 65
Scotland, immigrants from, 20
Scott, Winfield, 53
Scott county, 53, 72, 73
Scott's branch, 68
Seacock swamp, 30
Seaward, John, 11
Seneca creek, 39
Shenandoah county, 35, 49, 58, 62
Shenandoah (Sherrendo) river, 23, 35, 50, 62, 63
Shenandoah valley, 23, 51, 64
Shepherd, David G., 65
Harvey, 65
Shires, (political division), 3, 5
Shock, Jacob, 61
Shooting creek, 43
Showlands, John, 17
Shuler's island, 58
Shuler's run, 58
Simpson's creek, 17, 47
Sinking creek, 64
Sinking creek valley, 71
Sizer, Daniel, 71

Skiffe's (Keith's) creek, 6
Skimeno (Skimino) creek, 14
Skinquarter creek, 20
Sleepy creek mountain, 55
Smith's river, 46
Smyth, Alexander, 58, 59
Smyth county, 58, 59, 76
Snow creek, 19
Sonners, Isaac, 70
South Anna river, 17
South branch, 47
South mountain, 39
South river, 34, 58
Southam parish, 39
Southampton, Henry Wriothesley, 2d Earl of, 5, 28
Southampton county, 27, 28, 30
Southwark parish, 30
Spencer, West Va., 73
Spessard, John, 64
Spotswood, Alexander, 18, 19, 20, 27, 49, 64
Spotsylvania county, 19, 20, 21, 23
Stafford county, 15, 21, 31
Stafford county, England, 15
Stanard, William Glover, 37
Staunton, 37
Staunton and Parkersburg turnpike, 72
Staunton river, 28, 33, 38, 42, 43
Steel, George, 75
Steele's mill, 40
Steer creek, 61
Stephens, John, Jr., 70
Stephenson, Adam, 69
Stith, William. *History of Virginia*, 2, 7
Stock creek, 49, 73
Stone Coal gap, 71
Stott's ferry, 38
Stover, Jacob, 23
Strait Stone creek, 33
Strasburg, 62
Stratford Hall, 13, 21
Surrey county, England, 14
Surry county, 14, 22, 29, 30
Surveyors of land, 3
Susan Constant (*Ship*), 1
Susquehanna river, 71

100

DATE DUE